JEWELRY&GEMS
THE BUYING GUIDE
How to Buy Diamonds, Pearls, Precious and Other Popular Gems with Confidence and Knowledge

Antoinette L. Matlins & A.C. Bonanno, F.G.A., P.G., M.G.A.

GEMSTONE PRESS
SOUTH WOODSTOCK, VERMONT

DISTRIBUTED BY

VAN NOSTRAND REINHOLD
_____New York

Publishing History

1984, First Edition, Hardcover, Published by Crown Publishers, Inc., New York as *The Complete Guide To Buying Gems.*

1985, First Edition, Hardcover, Second Printing

1987, Second Edition, Softcover, Revised, Updated, Expanded, Published by GemStone Press, South Woodstock, Vermont as *Jewelry & Gems: The Buying Guide.*

1988, Second Edition, Softcover, Second Printing

1989, Second Edition, Softcover, Third Printing

Library of Congress Cataloging-in-Publication Data

Matlins, Antoinette Leonard.
  Jewelry & gems.
  Bibliography: p.
  Includes index.
    1. Jewelry—Purchasing.   2. Precious stones—Purchasing.   I. Bonanno, Antonio C.   II. Title.
III. Title: jewelry and gems.
TS756.M28   1987   736'.2   87-23807
ISBN 0-943763-01-0 (pbk.)

Cover photograph courtesy of
 ©1985

Book design by Dana Sloan

10 9 8 7 6 5 4

Manufactured in the United States of America

GemStone Press
A Division of LongHill Partners, Inc.
Long Hill Road, P.O. Box 276
South Woodstock, Vermont 05071
(802-457-4000)

To Ruth Bonanno,
who had nothing—and everything—
to do with it

All of the charts that appear here were especially designed and executed for use in this book; however, in some cases, charts from other publications were used as inspiration and reference. Grateful acknowledgment is given to the following for use of their charts as references:

The chart on page 26, "Three Standards for Proportioning," used with permission of the Gemological Institute of America, from their book, *The Jewelers' Manual*.

The chart on page 36, "Commonly Used Color-Grading Systems," © 1978 by Eric Bruton, from his book *Diamonds*, published by the Chilton Book Company, Radnor, Pennsylvania.

The chart on page 50, "Sizes and Weights of Various Diamond Cuts," with permission of the Gemological Institute of America, from their book, *The Jewelers' Manual*.

The chart on page 51, "Diameters and Corresponding Weights of Round, Brilliant-Cut Diamonds," with permission of the Gemological Institute of America, from their book, *The Jewelers' Manual*.

The chart on page 62, "Diamond and Diamond Look-Alikes," with permission of the Gemological Institute of America, from their publication *Diamond Assignment No. 36*, page 27.

Grateful acknowledgement is also given to the following for permission to use the photographs which appear after page 110:
The photographs of diamonds (Plates 1, 2, and 3), courtesy of the Diamond Information Center. The remaining photographs (Plates 4-9), © 1983 Carole Cutner, Carole Cutner Photography, London.

Contents

Part One

Part Two

v

Part Three

Part Four

Color plates follow page 112

1. Fancy diamonds
2. A fine, round, brilliant-cut diamond
3. Diamonds showing popular fancy cuts
4. Yellow-colored gemstones
5. Red-colored gemstones
6. Green-colored gemstones
7. Blue-colored gemstones
8. Tourmaline bracelet
9. Popular birthstones

Acknowledgments

Although we are closely related (father and daughter), we found that in many cases we had different people to thank and different reasons for thanking them. For this reason, we have decided to express our gratitude separately.

I first thank my father, who shared with me in this task, who inspired me as a child and filled me with awe and wonder, and who gave so generously of his knowledge. In addition, I want to thank my husband, Stuart Matlins, for his support, encouragement, and willingness to suffer many hours of loneliness as I labored through the days and nights; and my wonderful daughter, Dawn Leonard, for her love, support and independence, without which I would never have found the time or focus to attempt this undertaking.

Antoinette Leonard Matlins

I thank Dr. William F. Foshag, Edward P. Henderson, and James H. Benn, all of the United States National Museum, whose generosity and patience started me as a young teenager in this field; Miss Jewel Glass, Dr. Hugh Miser, Dr. Clarence Ross, Joseph Fahey, all of the United States Geological Survey, Dr. Frank Hess, of the United States Bureau of Mines, and Dr. Hatton Yoder, of the Geophysical Laboratory of the Carnegie Institution, for their interest and help as my interest and thirst for knowledge grew.

Antonio C. Bonanno, F.G.A., M.G.A., P.G.

Together, we would like to express our appreciation to the following for their assistance in creating this book:

Karen Bonanno Ford, F.G.A., P.G.
Kathryn L. Bonanno, F.G.A., P.G.
Kenneth E. Bonanno, F.G.A., P.G.

Preface

In working with my own clients to acquire gemstones and jewelry since this book was first published in 1984, they have pointed out that most people buy "jewelry" and not "gemstones." Because the book offers so much practical advice and money-saving tips about buying jewelry, they urged me to change the title. So, in this edition *The Complete Guide to Buying Gems* has been changed to *Jewelry & Gems: The Buying Guide*.

Consumer and professional response to the book has been very gratifying. Almost 14,000 hardcover copies are in circulation. We have received hundreds of letters, phone calls and in-person comments about the helpfulness and interesting information it provides. We thank you for encouraging us to make the book more widely available by bringing out this softcover edition.

We have taken the opportunity of this softcover edition to update the price guides for diamonds and colored gemstones and, in light of the increase in both the popularity and price of pearls, to add a price guide for them in the "Guide to Popular Gems and Their Prices."

Also, we want to take this opportunity to comment further on gem invest-ment, taking into account major developments since the original manuscript was written in 1980.

In Chapter 19, "A Word About Investment," we did not (and still do not) recommend gems as an investment for the average investor. However, we discussed some investment pros and cons because, whether or not we thought it wise, "investment" was a word the public was applying all-too-frequently to gem and jewelry purchases when we wrote the book.

During the late 1970s gem prices were pushed to unprecedented levels. Numerous "gemstone investment companies" and fraudulent "investment" schemes appeared. Then, prices for diamonds plummeted in 1981, followed shortly thereafter by price declines for other gems. Consumer losses were significant. Many of the gem investment companies went out of business.

We thought people had learned that investing in gems is not a "quick and easy" way for the unsophisticated investor to make money; it is an area that requires extensive knowledge and a long-term commitment. The gem market stabilized and strengthened as people returned to buying "jewelry"—beautiful things to wear, to give as a token of love or as a special memento.

Early in 1985, however, we saw indications of renewed interest in speculative gemstone investment. Today, those indications seem even stronger. Reports showing that as long-term investments (over 10 years) gems have outperformed many other investment vehicles appear in many publications. *The figures are very attractive, but the often simplistic presentation of rewards without full discussion of the risks alarms us.*

Gemstone investment can be profitable, but we cannot overemphasize the need to *exercise extreme caution*. Most buyers lack the expertise to know what they are buying for investment purposes. Few buyers have access to pricing information that will enable them to evaluate the investment merit of a purchase. Most buyers do not have the means to dispose of gems at attractive prices when they decide to or have to sell. It is vital to understand that most gemstones bought by the average consumer are purchased at retail prices but are sold at wholesale prices or below. It usually takes many years for the current wholesale price to exceed some previous retail price.

In light of our concern about a resurgence of interest in gemstone investment on a large scale, and the growing potential for renewed speculation, we would like to refer any reader seriously considering gem investment to our article (written after publication of this book), "The Hardest Asset: Diamonds and Other Gemstones" (*Personal Investor*, September 1985). This article is much broader in scope than the Investment chapter in our book and was written for the serious investor, not the average consumer. A copy of the article may be obtained from GemStone Press, Box 276, South Woodstock, VT 05071 for $5.00 (to cover reproduction, postage and handling).

Whatever your interest in gems, we hope they give you the pleasure and joy they have given us throughout the years. And we hope that this book will add new "facets" to your understanding and appreciation.

Antoinette Leonard Matlins
South Woodstock, Vermont
October 1987

Introduction

Throughout history, gems have been a much-sought-after commodity. Their beauty, rarity, and inherent "magical powers" have made them the symbol of kings, the symbol of power, the symbol of wealth, and in more recent history the symbol of love. Every civilization, every society, grandly exhibits man's fascination with and desire to possess these beautiful gifts of nature.

As the growth of the American jewelry business attests, we are no different from our ancestors. We too share the fascination, appreciation, and desire to possess beautiful gems. If history serves as a sound indicator of taste, we can rest assured that the lure of gems will be just as great in future generations. At least once in a lifetime nearly every American has an occasion to buy or receive a gem.

The experience of purchasing a gem can be a magical one. It can be filled with excitement, anticipation, and pleasure—and it is to that end that this book is dedicated. The purpose of this book is to provide a basic but complete consumer's guide to buying a gem, whether it be for one's own personal pleasure, to give, or for investment. It is designed and written for a wide market—husbands, wives, or parents buying gems as gifts for loved ones for some special occasion; young couples looking for an engagement ring to last a lifetime; tourists, business travelers, and service men and women traveling throughout the world hoping to pick up real bargain gems while they are near the mines; investors looking for a hedge against inflation; or those who are simply interested in gems, perhaps as a hobby. It will explain the variables that affect cost, provide information regarding fraudulent practices, provide lists of relevant questions that should be asked of a jeweler. It will not make you a gemologist, but it will make you a smart shopper who will be able to derive pleasure from what can become a truly exciting, interesting, and safe experience.

From the time I was a small child, I had the pleasure of being surrounded by beautiful gems and had a unique opportunity to learn the gem business. Having a father who was a well-known gemologist, appraiser, and collector, I was able to spend hours marveling at stones—those in his own private collection as well as those brought to him to be professionally appraised.

Dinner conversation usually centered on the day's events at my father's office. Sometimes he would thrill us with an account of a particularly fine or rare gem he had had the pleasure of identifying or verifying. But too often the subject would turn to some poor, unknowing consumer who had been victimized. It might have been a soldier who thought he had purchased genuine sapphires while in Asia, and learned sadly that they were either glass or synthetic; or a housewife who bought a "diamond" ring, only to learn that the stone was a white sapphire or zircon. It might have been a doctor who thought he had purchased a fine, natural canary diamond as a gift for his wife, who learned to his dismay that the beautiful bright yellow color was not natural at all, but the result of special treatment, and not worth anywhere near what he had paid for it.

One story in particular illustrates especially well how complex the gem business can be.

One day an average-looking elderly woman came into my father's office with a green stone she wanted identified and appraised. She had already taken the stone to a well-known jeweler who also had an excellent reputation as a gemologist-appraiser. The jeweler told her that the stone was a tourmaline worth only a few hundred dollars. She was very disappointed, since it was a family heirloom that she had believed for many years was a fine emerald. Her own mother had assured her of the fact. When she questioned the jeweler about its being an emerald, he laughed and told her that was impossible. He was the expert, so she accepted his appraisal, as most people would.

Many months later, at the insistence of a friend who knew of my father's reputation from the curator of the Smithsonian's gem collection, she sought my father's opinion. In fact, it was a genuine emerald, and one of the finest my father had ever seen. He could barely contain his excitement about the stone. It was worth about $60,000 even then, which was about twenty years ago. Fortunately, the old woman learned its true identity and value before it was too late.

My first response upon hearing the story was anger at the "dishonest" jeweler, but, as my father explained, he was not dishonest. Dad actually went to see this man, because he knew his reputation was good. The jeweler discussed the stone with my father, and it became clear that he genuinely believed it to have been a tourmaline. Based upon the woman's "ordinary" appearance and the complete absence of any of the flaws so characteristic of emerald, he drew the immediate conclusion that the stone could only be a green tourmaline. His experience with emeralds was limited to those of lesser quality, with their telltale inclusions, so he was completely incorrect in his identification of this unusually fine stone. He was not dishonest—hoping to pick up a steal—merely mistaken.

This anecdote illustrates the danger consumers frequently face when they come to buy gems. They are vulnerable not only to *intentional* fraud but also to *unintentional* misrepresentation resulting from a jeweler's lack of experience and knowledge. The very person on whom one would naturally rely—the reputable jeweler—sometimes lacks sufficient knowledge about the gems he is selling. Fortunately, educational institutions such as the Gemological Institute of America (in New York and Los Angeles) and the Columbia School of Gemology (near Washington, D.C.) are helping to rectify this situation. More and more, reputable jewelers are concerned with increasing their own knowledge and that of their salespeople, not only to protect their valued customers, but also to protect themselves!

Another story that occurred only this year, proves how rewarding education can be. A former student of my father's was visiting in a midwestern city. She decided to go to some pawnshops to kill time and in one shop discovered a beautiful diamond-and-emerald ring. The pawnbroker told her that the diamonds were unusually fine quality, which her examination confirmed. The ring was also beautifully designed, with outstanding workmanship. The question she had was whether the emerald was genuine or synthetic. Something about the stone made her feel it was not genuine. But she didn't have the right equipment with her to be sure. The price, $500, was not more than the diamonds and the gold setting alone should have cost, indicating that the pawnbroker believed the emerald was synthetic. But since she liked the ring, and the price was fair based on the value of the setting and diamonds, she was willing to take a chance that it might in fact be genuine. Upon her return to Washington she brought the ring to my father's lab, where they proceeded immediately to examine the emerald. It was genuine, and she sold the ring to a New York dealer for $18,000. The pawnbroker lost because of his lack of knowledge; the student profited because of her knowledge. I might add that in this case the knowledgeable New York dealer also profited, because he recognized an opportunity to get a good buy (since it was being offered at less than the current dealer cost), and he probably sold it for about $24,000 to a fine jewelry store, where it was probably offered to one of their valued clients for a fair price of $35,000 to $40,000.

As the result of my father's long experience in the gem business, and my own in the last seven years, I have felt for some time that a book about gems written just for the consumer was desperately needed. The cost of gems is greater than ever before, and projections indicate that prices will continue to rise. Over the past ten years the price of diamonds has shown a significant increase. The cost of precious colored stones such as sapphires, emeralds, and rubies can go as high as $10,000 per carat for top-quality stones. In addition, the price of many semiprecious stones, including many of the most popular birthstones, has increased as much as 100 percent. (During one recent eighteen-month period the price of aquamarine doubled to over $1,000 per carat for fine stones, and ruby-colored spinel now can bring more than $2,500 per carat.)

Furthermore, the gem market is expanding at a rapid rate because many consumers are buying gems not only for sentimental reasons such as engagements, weddings, and anniversaries, but solely for the sake of investment. More than two hundred gem-investment companies have been formed since the mid-1970s. Salomon Brothers, in a report issued in June 1979, ranked diamond high (eighth) in overall investment performance over an eleven-year period, ahead of oil, farmland, housing, foreign exchange, stocks, and bonds. With greater and greater frequency, reputable publications such as *Barrons*, the *Wall Street Journal*, the *New York Times*, *Business Week*, and *Time* are running advertisements for gem investment.

Thus, in a market where jewelers and gem dealers are often not as knowledgeable as they should be, where the price of gems continues to soar, and where consumers consider ever more frequently using gems as a source of sound investment, the gem buyer must begin to become more informed. Training a consumer to be an expert in gems is an impossible task through the medium of a book (one needs special training), but we can provide some basic information to make buying gems—for either fun or investment—a more pleasurable, less vulnerable experience.

The Complete Guide to Buying Gems covers everything you, the consumer, need to know before buying any of the most popular gems. Included are:

- Basic information about how to look at gems
- Basic information on factors that affect value
- Information regarding the most frequently encountered types of fraud and misrepresentation, and how to protect yourself
- Lists of questions to ask your jeweler before buying a specific stone
- Information on how to select a reputable jeweler or appraiser

I hope you will find as much pleasure as I have found in getting to know gems, and that your future purchases will be happy ones.

Antoinette Leonard Matlins
New York City
October 1980

Part One

Getting to Know Gems

1

Becoming Intimate with Gems

Gems should never be bought as a gamble—the uneducated consumer will always lose. This is a basic rule of thumb. The best way to take the gamble out of buying a particular gem is to familiarize yourself with the gem. While the average consumer can't hope to make the same precise judgments made by a qualified gemologist, whose scientific training and wealth of practical experience provide a far greater data base from which to make his judgments, the consumer can learn to judge a stone as a "total personality," and learn what the critical factors are—color, perfection, cut, brilliance, and weight—and how to balance them in judging the gem's value. Learning about these factors, and spending time in the marketplace looking, listening, and asking questions before going out to actually buy, will prepare you to be an intelligent buyer, rather than a potential victim.

Try to become intimate with the kind of stone you want to buy. Examine the stones owned by your friends, noting the difference in

3

shades of colors, brilliance, and cut. Go to a good, established jewelry store and ask to see fine stones. If the prices vary, ask why. Let the jeweler point out differences in color, cut, or brilliance, etc., and if he can't, go to another jeweler with greater expertise. Begin to develop an eye for the fine stone by looking, listening, and asking good questions.

Four key questions to ask yourself initially before you consider buying any stone are:

1. Is the color what you desire?
2. Is the shape what you want?
3. Does it have liveliness, or "zip"?
4. Can you afford it?

If you answer yes to all four questions, you are ready to consider the specific nature of the stone.

The Six Key Steps in Examining a Stone

1. *Whenever possible, examine stones unmounted.* They can be examined more thoroughly out of their settings, and defects cannot be hidden by the mounting or any side stones.
2. *Make sure the gem is clean.* If no professional means of cleaning the stone is available, breathe on the stone in a huffing manner in order to "steam" it with your breath and then wipe it with a clean handkerchief. This will at least remove the superficial film of grease.
3. *Hold the unmounted transparent stone so that your fingers touch only the girdle.* Putting your fingers on the table (top) and/or pavilion (bottom) will leave traces of oil, which will affect color and brilliance.

   The *careful* use of tweezers instead of fingers is recommended only if you feel comfortable using them. Make sure you know how to use them and get the permission of the owner before picking up the stone. It is easy for the stone to pop out of the tweezers and to become damaged or lost, and you could be held responsible.
4. *View the gem under proper lighting.* Many jewelers use numerous incandescent spotlights, usually recessed in dropped ceilings.

Some use special spotlights that can make any gemstone—even glass imitations—look fantastic.

Fluorescent lights may also adversely affect the color of gems. Diamonds will not show as much fire under fluorescent lighting, and colored gems, such as rubies, look much better in daylight or under incandescent light.

The light source should come from above or behind you, shining down and through the stone, so that the light traveling through the stone is reflected back up to your eye. Never hold the stone up to the light.

5. *Rotate the stone in order to view it from different angles.*
6. *If you are using a loupe, focus it both on the surface and into the interior.* To focus into the interior, shift the stone slowly, raising or lowering it, until you focus clearly on all depths within the stone. This is important because if you focus on the top only, you will miss any small flaws in the interior of the stone.

How to Use a Loupe

A loupe is a special type of magnifying glass. The use of the loupe can be very helpful in many situations, even for the beginner. With a loupe you can check a stone for chips or scratches or examine certain types of noticeable inclusions more closely. However, remember, even using a loupe, you will not have the knowledge or skill to be able to see or understand the many telltale indicators that an experienced jeweler or gemologist will be able to spot. No book can provide you with that knowledge or skill. Do not allow yourself to be deluded or let a little knowledge give you a false confidence or cockiness. Nothing will more quickly alienate a reputable jeweler or mark you faster as easy prey for the disreputable dealer.

The loupe (pronounced *loop*) is a very practical tool to use once you master it, and with practice it will become more and more valuable. The correct type is a 10×, or ten-power, "Triplet" and can be obtained from any optical supply house. The triplet lens is corrected for both distortion and color fringing.

You *must* use 10×, since only a 10× loupe is officially recognized as being strong enough to determine a stone's degree of perfection. *Any flaw that does not show up under 10× magnification is considered nonexistent.*

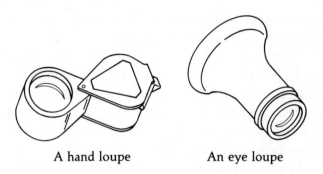

A hand loupe   An eye loupe

With a few minutes' practice you can easily learn to use the loupe. Here's how:

1. Hold the loupe between your thumb and forefinger of either hand.
2. Hold the stone or ring similarly in the other hand.
3. Bring both hands together so that the fleshy parts just below the thumbs are pushed together and braced by the lower portion of each hand just above the wrists (the wrist portion is actually a pivot point).
4. Now move the hands up to your nose or cheek, with the loupe as close to the eye as possible. If you wear eyeglasses, you do not have to remove them.

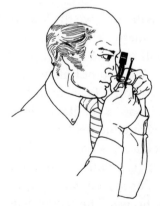

How to hold a loupe when examining a stone

5. Get a steady hand. With gems it's very important to have steady hands for careful examination. With your hands still

together and braced against your face, put your elbows on a table. (If a table isn't available, brace your arms against your chest or rib cage.) If you do this properly you will have a steady hand.

Practice with the loupe. Learn to see through the loupe clearly. A 10× loupe is difficult to focus initially, but with a little practice it will become easy. You can practice on any object that is difficult to see— the pores in your skin, the root of a strand of hair, a pinhead, or your own jewelry.

Play with the item being examined. Rotate it slowly, tilt it, tilt it back and forth while rotating it, look at it from different angles and different directions. It won't take long before you are able to focus it easily on anything you wish to examine.

What the Loupe Can Tell You

With practice and experience (and further education if you're really serious), a loupe can tell even the amateur a great deal. For a gemologist it can help determine whether the stone is natural, synthetic, glass, or a doublet (a composite stone, to be discussed later); it can help him see and identify characteristic flaws, blemishes, or cracks. In other words, it can provide the necessary information to know whether the stone is in fact what it is supposed to be.

For the beginner, it will be useful in determining the following:

1. *The workmanship that went into the cutting.* For example, is the symmetry of the stone balanced? Does it have the proper number of facets for its cut? Is the proportion good? Few cutters put the same time and care into cutting glass as they do into a diamond.
2. *Spotting chips, cracks, or scratches on the facet edges, planes, or table.* While zircon, for example, looks very much like diamond because of its pronounced brilliance and relative hardness, it chips easily. Therefore, careful examination of a zircon will often show chipping, especially around the table edges and the girdle. Glass, which is very soft, will often show scratches. Normal wear can cause it to chip or become scratched. Also, if you check around the prongs, the setter may even have

scratched it while simply bending the prongs to hold the stone.

In stones such as emeralds, the loupe can also help you determine whether or not any natural cracks are really serious— how close they are to the surface, how deep they run, how many are readily visible, etc.

3. *The sharpness of the facet edges.* Harder stones will have a sharp edge, or sharper boundaries between adjoining planes or facets, whereas many imitations are softer and under the loupe the edges between the facets are less sharp and have a more rounded appearance.

4. *Bubbles, inclusions, and flaws.* Many flaws and inclusions that cannot be seen with the naked eye are easily seen with the loupe. But remember, many are not easily seen unless you are very experienced. The presence of inclusions is not as serious in colored stones as in diamonds, and they don't usually significantly reduce the value of the stone. However, the *kind* of inclusions seen in colored stones can be important. They often provide the necessary key to positive identification, determine whether a stone is natural or synthetic, and possibly locate the origin of the stone, which may significantly affect the value. With minimal experience, the amateur can also learn to spot the characteristic bubbles associated with glass.

The loupe can tell you a great deal about the workmanship that went into cutting a gem. It can help you decide whether a gem is natural, a synthetic, a doublet, or glass. It can tell you whether the gem is what it's supposed to be, and it can tell you about inclusions or surface blemishes. But this takes lots of practice and experience.

In the following chapters relevant factors for the serious consumer will be discussed, but an understanding of at least the most basic points is really essential for the average consumer. Of greatest importance is learning how to look at a gem, even if you don't see all a gemologist will. Nonetheless, armed with a basic education, you will be a wise consumer.

2

Factors of Importance –an Overview

This chapter will discuss, in a general way, the basic factors that affect the appearance and value of any gemstone. Of primary importance in both diamonds and colored gems are *cut* and *proportion* of faceted stones. Faceted stones are stones on which a series of tiny flat planes (facets) have been cut and polished. (Nonfaceted stones are called *cabochons*. These will be discussed in detail in Part Three.)

In any stone, if the basic material is of good quality, the way in which it is cut will make the difference between a dull, lifeless stone and a beautiful, brilliant stone. In diamonds, the combination of cut (the shape of the stone) and its relative proportioning will provide the greatest influence on the stone's brilliance and fire. In colored gems, the perfection of the cut is not as important as it is with diamonds, but its proportioning remains critical because it will significantly affect the *depth of color* of the stone as well as its brilliance and liveliness.

The Cut of a Stone

When talking about the cut of a stone, you should be familiar with a few general terms that apply to all faceted stones. These various parts can vary in proportion to the rest of the stone and thus affect the stone's brilliance, beauty, and desirability.

Crown. The crown is also called the *top* of the stone. This is simply

9

the upper portion of the stone, the part above the girdle.

Girdle. The girdle is the edge or border of the stone.

Pavilion. The pavilion is the bottom portion of the stone, measuring from the girdle to the bottom point.

Culet. The culet is the lowest part or point of the stone. It may be missing in some stones, which can indicate damage, or, particularly with colored stones, it may not be part of the original cut.

Table. The table is the flat top of the stone and is the stone's largest facet, often called the face.

Table spread. This term is used to describe the width of the table facet, often expressed as a percentage of the total width of the stone.

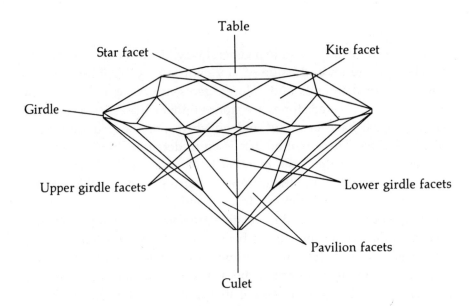

Terms for facets on a brilliant-cut stone

There are many popular cuts for gemstones. Each cut affects the overall look of the stone, but if the stone is cut well its brilliance and value endures no matter which cut you may choose. For the average consumer, which cut to choose is simply a matter of taste.

Some of the more popular cuts are:

Brilliant

Brilliant (side view)

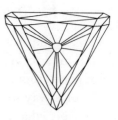

Trillion

Pear-shaped

Marquise or navette

Oval

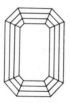

Emerald

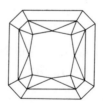

Radiant

Heart-shaped

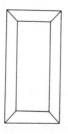

Baguette

Tapered baguette

How to Know If a Stone Is Cut Well

Look at the stone face up, through the top (table). This is the most critical area to view, since this is the one most often noticed. Is the color good from this direction? Is the table centered and symmetrical?

A quick way to check the symmetry of a round diamond is to look at the table edges. The lines should be straight, regular, and parallel to one another. The table edges should form a regular octagon, with the edges meeting in sharp points. If the lines of the table are wavy, the overall symmetry is not good, and the symmetry of the adjoining facets will also be affected.

| Table centered but not symmetrical | Table off-center and asymmetrical | Table centered and symmetrical—the ideal |

Next, look at the stone from the side. Note the proportion of the stone both above and below the girdle.

Crown too shallow (thin)   Crown too heavy (thick)

Ideal stone   Pavilion too shallow   Pavilion too deep (heavy)

The stone's proportion—whether it is too thin or too thick—will have a marked affect on its overall beauty. With colored stones, the relative terms of *thickness* or *thinness* vary greatly due to the inherent optical properties of different gemstones. As a general guide when considering colored stones, keep in mind these three points:

1. If the stone appears lively and exhibits an appealing color when viewed through the table, no matter how the proportion appears (thick or thin), it is usually correct and acceptable proportioning for that particular stone.
2. The depth of color (tone) will become darker as the stone is cut thicker, particularly if the bottom portion (pavilion) is deep and broad.
3. A stone's depth of color will become lighter as the stone is cut thinner. This is especially important when considering a pastel colored stone. A pastel stone should always have fairly deep proportioning.

The affects of cut and proportioning will be discussed in greater detail in Parts Two and Three, as the factors affecting cut and proportioning are somewhat different for diamonds and colored gems. It is important to become aware of general views and to begin to have a feeling about what looks "right."

The Setting

The setting you choose also is dictated primarily by your personal taste. Nevertheless, it is a good idea to be familiar with a few of the most common settings so that you have a working vocabulary and some idea of what is available.

Bezel setting. With a bezel setting, a rim holds the stone and completely surrounds the gem. Bezels can have straight edges, scalloped edges, or can be molded into any shape to accommodate the stone. The backs can be open or closed.

Prong setting. Prong settings are perhaps the most common type of setting. They come in an almost infinite variety; for example, four-prong, six-prong, and special styles, such as Belcher, Fishtail, and six-prong Tiffany.

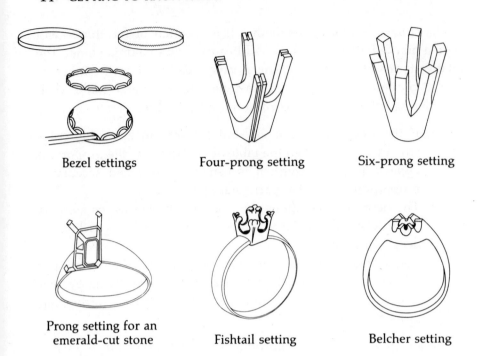

Bezel settings   Four-prong setting   Six-prong setting

Prong setting for an
emerald-cut stone   Fishtail setting   Belcher setting

Gypsy setting. In this type of setting, the metal at the top of the ring (around the stone) is much heavier than the shank. The stone is set flush into a hole at the top.

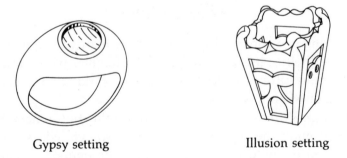

Gypsy setting   Illusion setting

Illusion setting. The illusion setting is used to make the mounted stone appear larger than it is.

Flat-top and bead settings. In a flat-top setting a faceted stone is placed into a hole in the flat top of the metal and then held in place by small chips of metal attached at the stone's girdle. Sometimes these metal

Flat-top or bead setting

Channel setting

Pavé setting

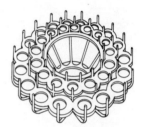

Cluster setting

chips are worked into small beads, so this setting is sometimes called a bead setting.

Channel setting. This setting is used extensively today, especially for wedding bands. The stones are set into a channel with no metal separating them. In some cases the channel can continue completely around the ring, so that the piece has a continuous row of stones.

Pavé setting. This setting is used for numerous small stones set together in a cluster with no metal showing through. The impression is that the piece is entirely paved with stones. The setting can be flat or domed-shaped, and can be worked so that the piece appears to be one larger stone.

Cluster setting. A cluster setting usually consists of one large stone and several smaller stones as accents. A cluster setting is designed to create a lovely larger piece from several small stones.

A Few Popular Ring Designs

Most of the settings we have just discussed apply not only to rings but to virtually any piece of jewelry, such as a pendant, bracelet, or pin. However, most often when consumers consider buying a gem they think in terms of buying a ring, particularly an engagement or wedding ring. Here are a few of the more popular styles.

Solitaire. The solitaire is precisely what its name denotes: a single large stone mounted in a setting. The stone can be of any cut (brilliant, emerald, pear, etc.), and the setting can be any one that sets off the stone to its best advantage (prong, illusion, fishtail, etc.).

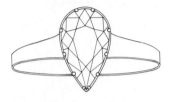

A solitaire ring

A large stone flanked by
two baguettes

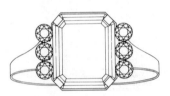

A large stone flanked by
three small stones

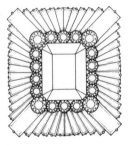

A ballerina-style setting

Large center stone flanked by smaller stones. There is no particular name for this type of ring, but it is a very common way to use stones beautifully. Again, the stones can be of any particular cut, and the side stones can be equally various. Usually, however, the smaller side stones are either round, baguette, or marquise.

Ballerina style. The ballerina style consists of one large stone surrounded by tapered baguettes, which are usually set in such a way that they seem to undulate. This is a very dramatic style and makes for an especially beautiful ring.

You are now equipped with a basic vocabulary for looking at gems. What follows is a more detailed accounting of the factors that affect the value of diamonds and then of colored gems. Some of this may appear complicated at first glance, but it won't be long before you are comfortable with the terms and fascinated by your knowledge.

Part Two

Diamonds

3

The Magic of Diamonds

The diamond has been one of the most coveted gems in history. Uncut diamonds adorned the suits of armor of the great knights; cut diamonds have adorned the crowns of kings and queens throughout the ages. Today the diamond is internationally recognized as a symbol of love and betrothal and is the recipient of increasing interest as a source for investment.

The diamond has been credited with many magical powers. At one time it was considered the emblem of fearlessness and invincibility. It was believed that mere possession of a diamond would endow the wearer with superior strength, bravery, and courage. It was also believed to drive away the devil and all spirits of the night.

In the 1500s it was believed to enhance the love of a husband for his wife. In the Talmud a gem believed to be a diamond (from its description) was worn by the high priest and served to prove innocence or guilt. If the accused was guilty, the stone grew dim; if innocent, it shone more brilliantly than ever.

The Hindus classed diamonds according to the four castes. The Brahmin diamond (colorless) gave power, friends, riches, and good luck; the Kshatriya (brown/champagne) prevented old age; Vaisya (the color of a "kodali flower") brought success; and the Sudra (a diamond with the sheen of a polished blade—probably gray or black)

19

brought all types of good fortune. Red and yellow diamonds were exclusively royal gems, for kings alone.

Diamonds have been associated with almost everything from producing sleepwalking to producing invincibility and spiritual ecstasy. Even sexual power has been strongly attributed to the diamond. There is a catch, however, to all the powers associated with it—one must find the diamond "naturally" in order to experience its magic, for it loses its powers if acquired by purchase. However, when offered as a pledge of love or friendship, its powers may return—hence its use in engagement rings, given in love.

What Is Diamond?

Chemically speaking, a diamond is the simplest of all gemstones. It is plain crystallized carbon—the same substance, chemically, as the soot left on the inside of a glass globe after the burning of a candle, the substance used in lead pencils.

The diamond differs from these in its crystal form, which gives it the desirable properties that have made it so highly prized—its hardness, which gives it its unsurpassed wearability, its brilliance, and its fire. (But note that while diamond is the hardest natural substance known, it can be chipped or broken if hit hard from certain angles; and if the girdle has been cut too thin it can be chipped with even a modest blow.)

The transparent colorless diamond is the most popular variety, but diamond also occurs in colors. When the color is prominent it is called a *fancy* diamond or *master fancy*, such as canary, yellow, brown, and lilac. Some colors are rarer than others. While diamond is frequently found in nice yellow and brown shades, colors such as pink, light green, and lavender occur much more rarely. Deep pink is especially rare. Reds, blues, and blacks have also been found, but the colors seen naturally in diamond usually tend to be pastel. Most colored diamonds historically have sold for more than their pure white counterparts, except for *very* pale yellow and brown varieties (which are the most abundantly found at the mines, and not considered fancy colors, but more properly off-white).

Fancy colored diamonds that obtained their color artificially, through exposure to certain types of radiation and heating techniques, are readily available. The bill of sale (and any accompanying certification, appraisal, etc.) should specify whether the color is natural or induced. If induced, the price should be much less, although the gem will often be just as beautiful as a natural.

How to Determine the Value of a Diamond

If we were to identify the factors that determine the value of a diamond in order of their importance, we would list them as follows:

1. Body color (color grade)
2. Degree of flawlessness (clarity grade)
3. Cut and proportion (often referred to as the *make*)
4. Carat weight

Each factor is a lesson in itself, and so we have devoted a chapter to each. For the sake of clarity, we have begun with a discussion of cut and proportion to familiarize you with the various terms used to describe the parts of the diamond.

4

The Importance of Cut and Proportion

The cut of a diamond and the proportioning of the cut—the make—are of extraordinary importance, because they have the greatest influence on the *fire* (variety and intensity of rainbow colors seen) and *brilliance* (liveliness, or sparkle) of the stone.

We will begin our discussion of diamond cut and proportion by discussing the round brilliant-cut stone, since this is the most popular cut. It usually displays the stone's qualities to their greatest potential, and is therefore the best "investment" cut.

The following diagram provides an illustration, in its simplest terms, of the effect of cut and proportion on fire and brilliance in a round brilliant-cut stone.

The importance of cut to brilliance

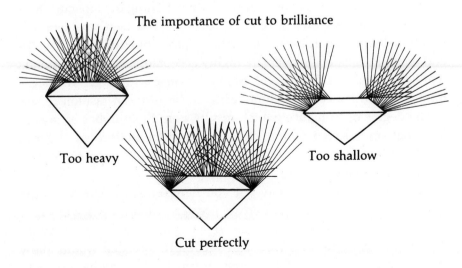

Too heavy

Too shallow

Cut perfectly

As a rule of thumb, if the top portion (*crown*) appears to be roughly one-third of the pavilion depth (distance from girdle to culet), the proportioning is probably acceptable.

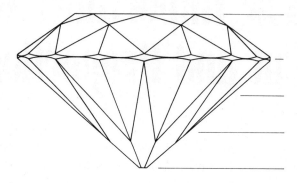

A well-proportioned stone

Types of Diamond Proportioning

There are several types of diamond proportioning that are currently used. They vary slightly in relation to width and depth percentages traditionally quoted as ideal. Nevertheless, the combinations of width and depth in each of them create highly acceptable stones. Diamonds that have smaller tables exhibit more fire; those with larger tables exhibit more brilliance. The latter seems to be more in fashion today.

The degree of brilliance (which results from the number of rays of light that are reflected from the back of the stone up through the top) and fire depend primarily on the table *spread* (width) and the crown and pavilion angles.

But, as common sense may tell you here, both can't excel in the same stone. A large table can create greater brilliance but will cause some reduction in fire; a small table area can increase fire but may reduce brilliance. The ideal would be a compromise that would allow the greatest brilliance and fire simultaneously. No one has come to agreement, however, on what the percentages should be, since some people prefer fire to brilliance, and vice versa. This is why there are several accepted types of proportioning found in diamond cut, and "best" is a matter of personal preference.

In 1919 Marcel Tolkowsky calculated that the best theoretical compromise was a cut in which the width of the table was 53 percent with a 40°45' pavilion angle. This means the width of the table equals 53 percent of the diameter of the stone (measuring across the stone at the girdle). He felt this provided the most vivid fire with the least loss of brilliance. The Tolkowsky cut provides the basis for the modern American ideal cut.

Today there are three recognized ideal proportions for round brilliant-cut diamonds:

1. Tolkowsky (also known as Standard American Ideal or American Cut)
2. Eppler (also known as European Cut)
3. Scan D.N. (Scandinavian Diamond Nomenclature, a popular European cut developed in 1970, used as a basis for grading in Scandinavia)

The basic differences between Tolkowsky's American cut and the other two can be seen in the table-spread variation and the height of the crown. All three are highly acceptable.

We must point out, however, that there are individual stones that do not adhere to these proportions but still show strong fire and brilliance. We have seen diamonds with table spreads to 64 percent and depth percentages to 62 percent that were highly acceptable, beautiful stones.

Once again, your eye will be responsible for making the final determination. In general, when you look at a diamond that has brilliance and fire, the cut and proportioning probably are acceptable. When a stone appears lifeless, seems to have a dead center, or a dark center, it probably results from poor cut and proportioning. The more time you take to look and compare diamonds of different qualities and prices, the better trained your eye will become to detect brilliance and fire, or lifelessness and dullness.

Tolkowsky

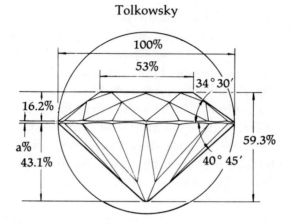

Eppler

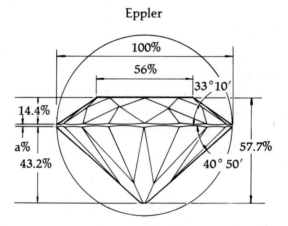

Scan D.N.

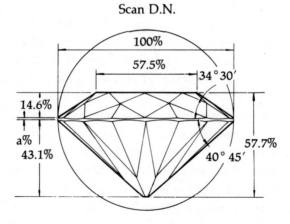

Three standards for proportioning—note the differences in table widths and crown heights.

Faulty Cuts

We have just discussed the most desirable cuts, but many errors can occur in the cutting that affect the appearance and the value of the stone. Here are a few faults to watch for. We used the brilliant cut as our example.

Look carefully for a sloping table or a table that is not almost perfectly perpendicular to the point of the culet.

The culet can frequently be the source of a problem. It can be chipped or broken, open or large (almost all modern cut stones have culets that come nearly to a point), or it can be missing altogether.

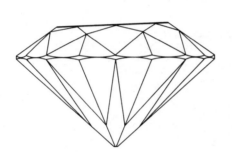

A brilliant-cut stone with a sloping table

Off-center culet

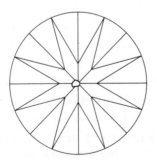

Open culet (viewed from the bottom)

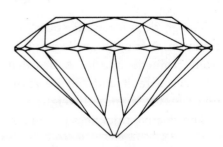

Broken or chipped culet

If repairs to chipped areas result in misaligned facets, the stone's symmetry will be off.

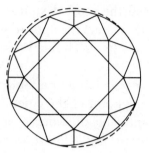

Poor symmetry

Sometimes, too, as a result of repair, an extra facet will be formed, often in the crown facets, but also on or just below the girdle. These extra facets may slightly affect the stone's brilliance.

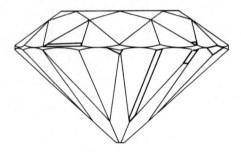

Stone with extra facets

Girdle Faults

The girdle is often the source of faults. *Bearded* or *fringed* girdles are common. A fringed girdle exhibits small radial cracks penetrating the stone from the girdle. A bearded girdle is similar but not as pronounced a fault and can be easily repaired by repolishing, without much loss in diamond weight.

The relative thickness of the girdle affects the value of the stone. If the girdle is too thick, it loses not only in aesthetic appeal but in dimension. Too much of the stone's weight will be in the girdle, so for its weight it will be smaller in diameter than another stone of comparable weight.

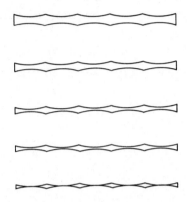

The gradations of girdle thickness

If the girdle is too thin, it will chip and nick more easily. These faults often occur under the prongs of a setting. Some can be easily removed by repolishing, with minimal loss in weight or value. If the chips are numerous, the entire girdle can be repolished.

The girdle can also be wavy, rough, or entirely out-of-round.

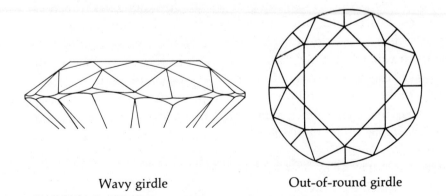

Wavy girdle   Out-of-round girdle

A *natural* is yet another fault that can occur in cutting. Usually, a natural results when a diamond cutter tries to get as large a diamond as possible from the rough stone. He overestimates and leaves a small portion of the natural surface of the rough crystal on the girdle. If this natural is no thicker than the thickness of the girdle and is not so long as to distort the circumference of the stone, most dealers consider it to be a minor defect.

Sometimes, if a natural is somewhat large and is slightly below the girdle, it can be polished off, producing an extra facet.

A natural at the girdle

Deviations in Other Popular Cuts

Within the popular fancy shapes, certain deviations have been established as standard. Some deviations fall within the "acceptable" range, while others do not. Moderate deviations will not affect the beauty or value of a stone; however, deviations that exceed acceptable tolerances can seriously reduce a stone's beauty and value.

One of the most obvious deviations in proportion in fancy shapes is the *bow tie*, or *butterfly* effect, a darkened area across the center or widest part of the stone, depending upon the cut. The bow tie is most commonly seen in the pear shape or marquise but may exist in any fancy shape. The degree of misproportion is directly related to the degree to which the bow tie is pronounced. The more pronounced the bow tie, the greater the degree of incorrect proportion.

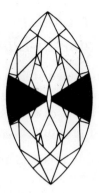

Marquise with a pronounced bow tie, or butterfly

As with the brilliant-cut diamond, fancy shapes can also be cut too broad or too narrow; and the pavilion can be too deep or too shallow.

Too broad

Too narrow

Culet too high

Culet too low

Open or misshapen culet

Pear-shaped stone,
cut correctly

To What Extent Do Cut and Proportion Affect Value in Diamonds?

Excellently cut and proportioned stones cost significantly more per carat than those that are not cut well. The following will give a very basic idea of the monetary effect of some of the most frequently encountered defects in cut and proportion.

- Table is not a reasonably accurate octagon—2 to 15 percent off
- Girdle is too thick—5 to 20 percent off
- Symmetry of crown facets off—5 to 15 percent on round, less on fancy cuts since defect is not so easily seen
- Asymmetrical culet—2 to 5 percent off
- Misaligned culet—5 to 25 percent off
- Stone too shallow—15 to 50 percent off
- Stone too thick—10 to 30 percent off
- Slightly thin crown—5 to 20 percent off
- Slightly thick crown—5 to 15 percent off

As you can see, there is a fairly wide range here, depending upon the severity of the error, and only an experienced professional can determine the extent to which the value of a given stone may be lessened. But a quick computation can show that a stone which suffers from several errors (which is fairly common) could certainly have its price per carat significantly reduced.

5

Body Color

How to Look at a Diamond to Evaluate Color

Before we can discuss color, it is important to know how to look at a diamond to evaluate color. Keep in mind that it is impossible to accurately determine color grade in a mounted stone, but even an amateur can learn to see color differences in an unmounted stone if the stone is viewed properly.

Because of the diamond's high brilliance and dispersion, the color grade cannot be accurately determined by looking at the stone from the top, or face-up, position. It is best to observe color by examining the stone through the pavilion with the table down. Use a flat white surface such as a white business card, or a *grading trough*, which can be purchased from a jewelry supplier or through the Gemological Institute of America (GIA). Next, view the stone with the pavilion side down and the culet pointing toward you.

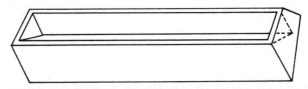

A grading trough, available in plastic for about $2

33

The following drawings show the best way to view loose diamonds.

Position 1. Place table-side down and view the stone through the pavilion facets.

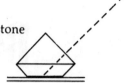

Position 2. Table-side down, view the stone through the plane of the girdle.

Position 3. Place the pavilion down with the culet pointing toward you. View the stone through the girdle plane.

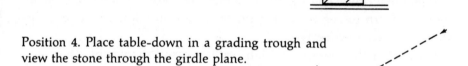

Position 4. Place table-down in a grading trough and view the stone through the girdle plane.

Position 5. Place pavilion-down in a grading trough, with the culet pointing toward you. View the stone through the pavilion facets.

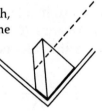

What Is Body Color?

When we discuss body color we are referring to how much yellow or brown tint is observable in the stone. We are not referring to the rare shades of blue, green, canary yellow, red, etc., that are designated in the trade as fancies.

Today, the color designation frequently used to grade an absolutely water-clear, colorless diamond is the letter D. This letter designation is part of a color-grading system introduced by the GIA and is used extensively in the diamond trade. The GIA classification progresses from D, the finest classification on this scale (colorless), through the alphabet to Z, getting progressively yellower. The grades, D, E, F are exceptionally fine and are the only grades that should be referred to as colorless. (Technically, E and F are not colorless since they possess a trace of yellow, but the color is so slight that referring to them as colorless is acceptable.)

A diamond classified D has the finest possible color. It is essentially colorless and considered the most desirable. (There are colorless diamonds with a slight tint of blue, which are more valuable, but these are not in the GIA grading classification.) These D stones are becoming very rare, and a significant premium is paid for them. A diamond classified as having E color also possesses a very fine color, and we must point out that it is extremely close to D on this scale, almost indistinguishable from D except to the very experienced, but nonetheless costs significantly less per carat.

F is also close to E, but shows a greater gradation in color than that observed between D and E.

What Color Grade Is Most Desirable for the Consumer?

For the average consumer, the colors D, E, and F can all be grouped as very fine and may be referred to as "colorless," "gem," or "gem white," as they are often described by diamond dealers. G and H may be referred to as "fine white." These grades are all considered to be very good, and good for investment. Depending on size and flaws, grade I may also be acceptable for investment, but as a general rule we do not recommend investing in color grades beyond I, since grades J–Z are more limited in their resale potential. This does not mean, however, that diamonds having color grades less fine than I aren't beautiful or desirable. They can make beautiful, highly desirable jewelry. But the *investor* should avoid stones with color grades below I.

The system of the GIA and that of the American Gem Society

COMMONLY USED COLOR-GRADING SYSTEMS

The GIA and AGS are the most commonly used systems in the U.S.A. GIA is becoming the most favored. In addition, note that these systems indicate a greater number of classifications, providing greater precision in the grading. They are more stringent than any other system. The interval sizes are an indication of the degree of rarity only.

CIBJO stands for the International Confederation of Jewelry, Silverware, Diamonds, Pearls, and Stones. Participating member nations who use this scale include: Austria, Belgium, Canada, Denmark, Finland, France, Great Britain, Italy, Japan, Netherlands, Norway, Spain, Sweden, Switzerland, United States, and West Germany.

HRD uses a system applied by the Belgian "Hoge Raad voor Diamant" (Diamond High Council). The use of the term *Blue White* is discouraged today since it is usually misleading.

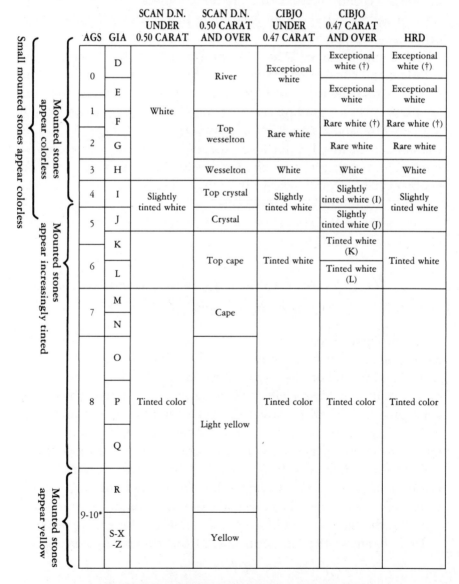

AGS	GIA	SCAN D.N. UNDER 0.50 CARAT	SCAN D.N. 0.50 CARAT AND OVER	CIBJO UNDER 0.47 CARAT	CIBJO 0.47 CARAT AND OVER	HRD
0	D	White	River	Exceptional white	Exceptional white (†)	Exceptional white (†)
	E				Exceptional white	Exceptional white
1	F		Top wesselton	Rare white	Rare white (†)	Rare white (†)
2	G				Rare white	Rare white
3	H		Wesselton	White	White	White
4	I	Slightly tinted white	Top crystal	Slightly tinted white	Slightly tinted white (I)	Slightly tinted white
5	J		Crystal		Slightly tinted white (J)	
6	K	Tinted color	Top cape	Tinted white	Tinted white (K)	Tinted white
	L				Tinted white (L)	
7	M		Cape	Tinted color	Tinted color	Tinted color
	N					
	O					
8	P					
	Q		Light yellow			
9-10*	R					
	S-X -Z		Yellow			

Left-side brackets (top to bottom): Small mounted stones appear colorless · Mounted stones appear colorless · Mounted stones appear increasingly tinted · Mounted stones appear yellow

*AGS grade "9" corresponds to GIA "R,S,T,U" inclusive.
AGS grade "10" corresponds to GIA "V,W" inclusive.

(AGS) are the most commonly used systems for grading color in the United States, with the GIA system becoming the more favored. Note that these systems include a greater number of classifications than other systems, providing greater precision in their grading.

What Extent Does the Color Grade Affect Value?

To an untrained eye, discerning the difference in color from D down to H in a mounted stone—without direct comparison—is almost impossible. Nevertheless, the difference in color greatly affects the value of the diamond. A 1-carat, flawless, excellently proportioned D diamond sold retail at one time for over $100,000, while the same stone with an I color sold for only $13,000.

This sounds complicated, but the range of color will become clear to you the moment you begin looking at stones. It is our intention to inform you of the variations so that you will be watchful when you go to purchase a stone.

What Is a Premier?

At this point we should discuss a type of diamond that is not encountered often, but often enough to warrant a brief discussion. This type of diamond is called a *premier.*

This diamond has an inherent property that gives it a blue or bluish tint when examined in daylight (sometimes a jeweler will say, "Take it outside and look at it"), or under a fluorescent light source, which many jewelers use for lighting in their stores. (Some diamonds that are not premier may also exhibit a blue tint when viewed directly under a fluorescent lamp, which may cause the color to appear several grades better than it actually is. This is one reason why the stone should be appraised by a qualified gemologist.) A premier diamond will not display this blue color *except* when exposed to the ultraviolet rays present in daylight and fluorescent tubes. This means that if you wear your premier diamond to a dinner party where there is candle-light or normal incandescent lighting, the blue will be totally gone and your diamond might have a yellow tint that you never noticed before.

Furthermore, the premier diamond will have, coupled with the blue coloration, a degree of yellow (in the jewelry trade yellow is termed *cape*) in its body color. This is important for you to know for two reasons: Since the blue tends to mask the yellow to some degree, you may be misled as to the color gradation and pay more than the gem is worth; the coupling of the bluish coloration with the yellow usually gives the stone some degree of murkiness, milkiness, or oiliness.

The blue tint is the result of the stone's degree of fluorescence. Misgrading the body color, which could be costly to you, can be avoided if a knowledgeable appraiser tests the stone to determine its degree of fluorescence, which will then enable him to color-grade it accurately.

The price of a premier varies depending on the degree of cape and murkiness, as well as the other three variables—cut, clarity, and carat weight.

Some Plain Talk About Fancies

Let's spend a moment discussing colored diamonds. Diamonds have been found to occur naturally in almost every color and shade—blue, red, green, yellow, lavender, pink, gunmetal blue, coffee brown, and black. The color can be intense or very pale.

These are very expensive because they are rare—some more than others. The most common fancy colors are shades of yellow (very intense, bright yellow called "canary"), orange and brown. Among the most rare and most valuable are the reds and blues; and the least valuable (yet still expensive) are the blacks.

One must be aware, however, that it is possible with the use of sophisticated radiation technology to alter poor-quality brownish and yellowish diamonds so that they become beautiful fancy colored stones. These should sell for much less than their naturally occurring counterparts. Unfortunately, this is not always the case. Sometimes a jeweler may buy a fancy colored stone that has been represented as a natural when in fact it is a cheaper, treated stone, and then pass it on to the consumer unintentionally. But there are tests—spectroscopic examination, electroconductivity, and ultraviolet response—that differentiate the natural from the treated colored diamond when administered by a qualified gemologist.

Special Tips on the Subject of Color

Keep It Clean If You Want Your Stone's Color Exhibited to Its Best

Particularly when considering purchasing an old diamond ring, note whether the ring is impacted with dirt accumulated by years of use. If it is, there is a possibility that the diamond will have a better color grade than it may appear to have at first glance. This is due to the fact that the dirt may contain varying amounts of fatty deposit (dishwasher grease, cosmetics, etc.), which has a tendency to yellow with age. Since this dirt is in contact with the back side of the diamond, it will have an adverse affect on the color, making it appear yellower than it actually is.

The same applies to your own diamond, so keep it clean in order to see and enjoy its full beauty.

White or Yellow Gold Setting?

The color of the setting in which your stone is placed can affect one's perception of the color of your stone—sometimes adversely and sometimes beneficially.

A diamond with good color that is going to be mounted in a yellow gold ring should be held or secured by either prongs or a bezel made from a white metal (white gold, platinum, or palladium). The color will appear less fine in a completely yellow setting.

On the other hand, if the diamond you choose tends to be yellower than you'd like, mounting in yellow gold with yellow gold prongs may make the stone appear whiter in contrast to the strong yellow of the gold.

The yellow gold environment may mask the degree of yellow in a yellow diamond, or it may give a colorless diamond an undesirable yellow tint. The setting can also affect future color grading should you ever need an updated insurance appraisal. This is important for you to know, and your appraiser, if knowledgeable, should certainly take the setting into consideration when color grading.

6

The Effect
of Flaws

Flaw classification is one of the most important criteria for determining the value of a diamond. The major grading system used in the United States is the GIA system. There are several other systems in use, but most American jewelers use GIA because it indicates a greater number of classifications and thereby provides greater precision in determining the flaw grade. The GIA system is therefore considered the most stringent.

Four Commonly Used Flaw Grading Systems

There are four systems that are commonly used for grading flaws. These are:

1. CIBJO (International Confederation of Jewelry, Silverware, Diamonds, Pearls, and Stones). Participating member nations who use this scale include Austria, Belgium, Canada, Denmark, Finland, France, Great Britain, Italy, Japan, Netherlands, Norway, Spain, Sweden, Switzerland, United States, and West Germany.
2. Scan D.N. (Scandinavian Diamond Nomenclature)
3. GIA (Gemological Institute of America)
4. AGS (American Gem Society)

Basically these systems grade the stone for its imperfections, both internal and external. Imperfections are called *inclusions* when internal, *blemishes* when external. Flaws can be white, black, colorless, or even red or green in rare instances. The "flaw" grade is more commonly referred to as the "clarity" grade today. Clarity and flaw, however, may be used interchangeably.

The following chart shows the relationships among these four systems, plus a system commonly used in Belgium (HRD).

COMMONLY USED FLAW (CLARITY) SYSTEMS

CIBJO UNDER 0.47 CARAT	CIBJO 0.47 CARAT AND OVER	HRD	SCAN D.N.	GIA	AGS
Loupe clean	Loupe clean	Loupe clean	FL	FL	0
			IF (Internally Flawless)	IF	1
VVS	VVS_1	VVS_1	VVS_1	VVS_1	
	VVS_2	VVS_2	VVS_2	VVS_2	2
VS	VS_1	VS_1	VS_1	VS_1	3
	VS_2	VS_2	VS_2	VS_2	4
SI	SI_1	SI	SI_1	SI_1	5
	SI_2		SI_2	SI_2	6
Piqué I	Piqué I	P1	1st Piqué	I_1 (Imperfect)	7
					8
Piqué II	Piqué II	P2	2nd Piqué	I_2	9
Piqué III	Piqué III	P3	3rd Piqué	I_3	10

VV = Very, Very
 V = Very
 S = Slight or Small
 I = Inclusion or Included or Imperfect (Imperfection)

For example, VVS may be translated to mean Very, Very Slightly (Included); or Very, Very Small (Inclusion); or Very, Very Slightly (Imperfect). Some jewelers prefer to classify the stone as "very, very small inclusion" rather than "very, very slightly imperfect," because the former description may sound more acceptable to the customer. There is, in fact, no difference.

FL is the grade given to a stone that has no visible flaws, internal or external, when examined under 10× magnification. Only a highly qualified person will be able to determine this grade. Also, note that it is very difficult for most inexperienced customers to see flaws that may be readily observable to the experienced jeweler, dealer, or gemologist. (It is highly unlikely that one would be able to see any flaws even in SI grades, despite use of the loupe.) A flawless, colorless, correctly proportioned stone, particularly of 1 carat and up, is extremely rare and is priced proportionately much higher than any other grade. Some jewelers insist there is no such thing in existence today.

IF is the grade given to a stone with no internal flaws and with only minor external blemishes—nicks, or pits or girdle roughness, *not* on the table—that could be removed with polishing. These stones, in colorless, well-proportioned makes, are also rare and priced proportionately much higher than other grades.

VVS$_1$ and VVS$_2$ are grades given to stones with internal flaws that are very, very difficult for a qualified observer to see. These are also difficult grades to obtain, and are priced at a premium.

VS$_1$ and VS$_2$ are grades given to stones with very small inclusions difficult for a qualified observer to see. These stones are more readily available in good color and cut, and their flaws will not be visible except under magnification. These are excellent stones to purchase. SI$_1$ and SI$_2$ grades are given to stones with flaws that a qualified observer will see fairly easily under 10× magnification. They are more prevalent and so command a lower price, and their flaws *may* sometimes be visible without magnification when examined from the back side or laterally. They are still highly desirable for good jewelry, and may be good investments in the larger sizes (over 3 carats) if they have good color and a good cut.

The imperfect grades are given to stones in which the flaws may be seen by a qualified observer without magnification; they are readily available and are much less expensive. They are graded I$_1$, I$_2$, and I$_3$. (These grades are called 1st pique, 2nd pique, and 3rd pique in some classifications.) They may still be quite desirable if they have good color and cut, and so should not be eliminated by a prospective purchaser who desires lovely diamond jewelry. As a general rule, however, Imperfect grades should not be considered for investment because they will be difficult to resell and therefore do not appreciate in value as rapidly as better grades.

Types of Diamond Imperfections

There are basically two types of flaws: internal flaws, or inclusions; and external flaws, or blemishes. Among these two categories are any number of flaws. We will discuss some of those flaws here, so that you have a working vocabulary of diamond imperfections.

Internal Flaws or Inclusions

Pinpoint. This is a small, usually whitish (although it can be dark) dot that is difficult to see. A group of pinpoints is simply a cluster of pinpoint flaws, and cannot be classified as VVS. A cloud of pinpoints is hazy and is not easily seen.

Dark spot. This may be a small crystal inclusion or a thin, flat inclusion that reflects light like a mirror. It may also appear as a silvery, metallic reflector.

Colorless crystal. This is often a small crystal of diamond, although it may be another mineral. Sometimes it appears very small, sometimes large enough to substantially lower the flaw grade to SI_2 or even I_1. A small group of colorless crystals lowers the grade from possible VS_2 to I_3.

Cleavage. A small cleavage is a crack that has a flat plane, which if struck, could cause the diamond to split.

Feather. This is another name for a crack. A feather is not dangerous if it is small and does not break out through a facet. Thermoshock or ultrasonic cleaners can make it larger.

Bearding or girdle fringes. These are usually the result of hastiness on the part of the cutter while rounding out the diamond. The girdle portion becomes overheated and develops cracks that resemble small whiskers going into the diamond from the girdle edge. Sometimes the bearding amounts to minimal "peach fuzz" and can be removed with slight repolishing. Sometimes the bearding must be removed by faceting the girdle. Bearding can be classified as IF if it is quite minimal.

Growth or grain lines. These can be seen only when examining the diamond while slowly rotating it. They appear and disappear usually instantaneously. They will appear in a group of two, three, or four pale brown lines. If they cannot be seen from the crown side of the diamond and are small, they will not affect the grade adversely.

Knaat or twin lines. These are sometimes classified as external flaws because they appear as very small ridges, often having some type of geometrical outline; or as a small, slightly raised dot with a tail resembling a comet. These are difficult to see.

Laser treatment. Used today to make flaws less visible, this improves the stone aesthetically. For example, a black spot can be "vaporized" and will practically disappear. However, the laser holes can be seen with a 10× loupe, looking like fine straight white threads.

External Flaws or Blemishes

A small natural. These usually occur on the girdle and look like a rough, unpolished area. They appear to be scratch lines or small triangles called *trigons*. If a natural is no wider that the normal width of the girdle or does not disrupt the circumference of the stone, some jewelers will not consider it a flaw.

Often naturals are polished and resemble an extra facet, especially if they occur below the girdle edge.

A natural is a remnant of the original skin of the diamond, and is often left on the girdle showing that the cutter tried to cut the largest possible diameter from the rough.

Nick. This is a small chip, usually on the girdle, and can be caused by wear, especially if the girdle has been proportioned on the thin side. Sometimes a nick or chip can be seen on the edge of the facets where they meet. If small, the bruised corner can be polished, creating an extra facet. This usually occurs on the crown.

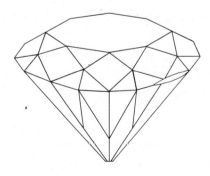

A natural at the girdle

Girdle roughness. This blemish appears as crisscrossed lines, brighter and duller finishing, and minute chipping. This can be remedied by faceting or repolishing.

Pits or cavities. Pits or holes on the table facet, especially if they are deep, will quickly lower the grade of the stone. Removing pits involves recutting the whole top of the stone, and can also shrink the stone's diameter.

Scratch. A scratch is usually a minor defect that can be removed with simple repolishing. Remember, however, that in order to repolish the stone, it must be removed from its setting, and then reset after it has been polished.

Polishing lines. Many diamonds exhibit polishing lines. If they appear on the pavilion side and are not too obvious, they do not lower the value. In some small diamonds these scratch lines can be obvious, and are usually the result of a badly maintained polishing wheel.

Abraded or rough culet. The culet has been chipped or poorly finished. This is usually a minor flaw.

How Does the Position of a Flaw Affect a Diamond's Grading and Value?

As a general rule, the position of any given inclusion will downgrade and devalue a diamond progressively more and more as indicated below:

- *If seen only from the pavilion side,* or clearly only from the pavilion side, it has the least adverse effect, since it is the least visible from the top.
- *If positioned near the girdle,* while perhaps more visible than described above, it is still difficult to see, and hardly noticeable from the top. This flaw can be easily covered with the prong of a setting.
- *Under any crown facet* (other than a star facet), except when near the girdle, a flaw is more easily visible.
- *Under a star facet,* a flaw will be much more easily visible.
- *Under the table* is the least desirable position, as it places the flaw where it is most noticeable, and may have the greatest effect on brilliance or fire (depending on size, color, etc.).

Sometimes a small black or white flaw may be in such a position that it is reflected within the stone. This can occur as a reflection to the opposite side of the stone, or, more unfortunately, it may reflect itself as many as *eight times* around the bottom or near the culet of the stone. A diamond with that flaw might otherwise be classified as a VS_1 or VS_2, but because of the eightfold reflection resulting from its unfortunate position, the flaw grade will be lowered.

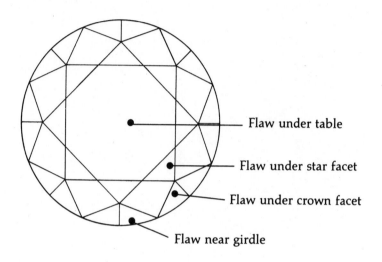

Flaw under table

Flaw under star facet

Flaw under crown facet

Flaw near girdle

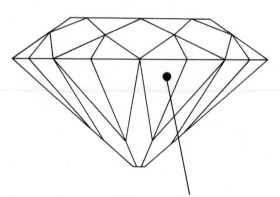

Flaw seen from the pavilion only

Remember, a diamond does not have to be flawless to be a very fine stone and to be of high value. We, personally, prefer a stone that might be slightly imperfect but has fine color and brilliance over a flawless stone with less sparkle and a less fine color. Color and bril-liance are considered to be the most important factors in terms of a stone's desirability. And remember: Even a diamond graded I_3 is still 97 percent clean!

7

Weight

What Is a Carat?

Diamonds are sold by the carat (ct)—not to be confused with *karat* (kt), which in the United States refers to gold quality.

The carat is a unit of weight, not size. (Since 1913 most countries have agreed that a carat weighs 200 milligrams, or ⅕ gram.) We wish to stress this point, since most people think that a 1-carat stone is a particular size. Most people, therefore, would expect a 1-carat diamond and a 1-carat emerald, for example, to look the same size or to have the same apparent dimensions. This is *not* the case.

If we compare a 1-carat diamond to a 1-carat emerald and a 1-carat ruby, we can easily illustrate this point. First, emerald weighs less than diamond and ruby weighs more than diamond. This means that a 1-carat emerald will look larger than a 1-carat diamond, and a 1-carat ruby will look smaller than a 1-carat diamond. Emerald, with a basic material that is lighter, will yield greater mass per carat; ruby, with its heavier basic material, will yield less mass per carat.

Let's look at this another way. Let's look at a 1-inch cube of pine wood, a 1-inch cube of aluminum, and a 1-inch cube of iron. The wood is like the emerald and weighs less than the aluminum, which is

SIZES AND WEIGHTS OF VARIOUS DIAMOND CUTS

Weight (ct)	Emerald	Marquise	Pear	Brilliant
5				
4				
3				
2½				
2				
1½				
1¼				
1				
¾				
½				

DIAMETERS AND CORRESPONDING WEIGHTS
OF ROUND, BRILLIANT-CUT DIAMONDS

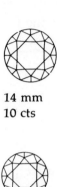

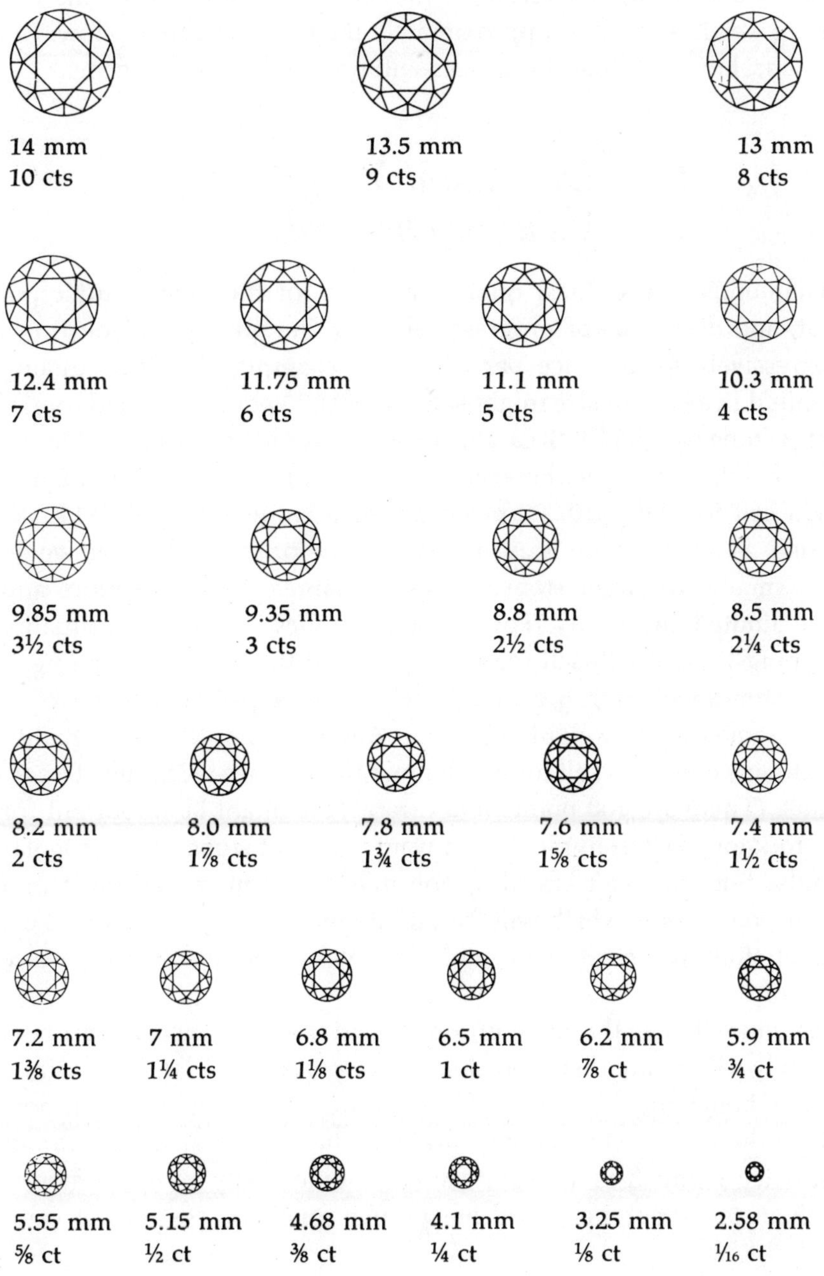

14 mm
10 cts

13.5 mm
9 cts

13 mm
8 cts

12.4 mm
7 cts

11.75 mm
6 cts

11.1 mm
5 cts

10.3 mm
4 cts

9.85 mm
3½ cts

9.35 mm
3 cts

8.8 mm
2½ cts

8.5 mm
2¼ cts

8.2 mm
2 cts

8.0 mm
1⅞ cts

7.8 mm
1¾ cts

7.6 mm
1⅝ cts

7.4 mm
1½ cts

7.2 mm
1⅜ cts

7 mm
1¼ cts

6.8 mm
1⅛ cts

6.5 mm
1 ct

6.2 mm
⅞ ct

5.9 mm
¾ ct

5.55 mm
⅝ ct

5.15 mm
½ ct

4.68 mm
⅜ ct

4.1 mm
¼ ct

3.25 mm
⅛ ct

2.58 mm
1⁄16 ct

like the diamond, and the iron, which is like the ruby, weighs the most, volume for volume. This is called density, mass, or specific gravity.

In diamond, the carat weight has come to represent particular sizes. These sizes are based upon the diamond being cut to ideal proportion (already discussed). Therefore, if properly cut, diamonds of the following weight should be approximately the size illustrated below. Remember, however, that these sizes will not apply to other gems.

How Does Carat Weight Affect Value in Diamonds?

Diamonds of the finest quality are sold for the highest price per carat, and diamonds of progressively less fine quality are sold for a progressively lower price per carat. For example, the finest-quality diamond in a certain size might sell for $50,000 per carat. Therefore, if such a stone weighed 1.12 carats, the stone would cost $56,000. On the other hand, a stone of the exact same weight, in a less fine quality, might sell for only $10,000 per carat, so it would cost only $11,200.

Also, as a rule, there is an increase in the price per carat as we go from smaller to larger stones, since the larger stones are more and more limited in supply. For example, stones of the same quality weighing ½ carat will sell for more per carat than stones weighing ⅓ carat; stones weighing ¾ carat will sell for more per carat than stones of the same quality weighing ½ carat. And stones of the same quality weighing 1 carat will sell for much more than stones weighing 90 to 96 points. (There are 100 points to a carat.) This might be important for you to know. For example, if you want a 1-carat stone of a particular quality, but you can't afford it, you may find you can afford it in a 90–96-point stone, which will for all intents and purposes look like a 1-carat stone when set. You might be able to get your heart's desire after all.

As you will see, the price of a diamond does not increase proportionately—there are disproportionate jumps. And the larger the stone (all else being equal in terms of overall quality), the more disproportionate the increase in cost per carat may be. A 2-carat stone will not cost twice as much as a 1-carat stone. It could easily be four times as much. A 5-carat stone would not be five times the cost of a 1-carat stone—it could easily cost as much as ten times per carat the price of the 1-carat stone.

Points

When discussing the carat weight of a diamond, jewelers often refer to the weight in terms of points. This is particularly true of stones under 1 carat. There are 100 points to a carat, so if a jeweler says that a stone weighs 75 points, he means it weighs $^{75}/_{100}$ of a carat, or ¾ carat. A 25-point stone is ¼ carat. A 10-point stone is $^{1}/_{10}$ carat.

What Is Spread?

The term *spread* is often used in response to the question "How large is this diamond?" But it can be misleading. Spread refers to the size the stone *appears* to be, based on its diameter. For example, if the diameter of the stone measured the same as you see in the Diamond Sizes chart (see pages 50 and 51), which represents the diameter of a perfectly proportioned stone, the jeweler might say it spreads 1 carat. But this does not mean it *weighs* one carat. It means it *looks* the same size as a perfectly cut 1-carat stone. It may weigh less or more, usually less.

Diamonds are usually weighed before they are set, as the jeweler must give you the exact carat weight since you are paying a certain price per carat. Note, also, that the price per carat for a fine stone weighing 96 points is much less than for one weighing 1 carat or more. So it is unwise to accept any "approximate" weight, even though the difference seems so slight.

As you can see here, it is also important when buying a diamond to realize that since carat refers to weight, the manner in which a stone is cut can affect its apparent size. A 1-carat stone that is cut shallow (see Chapter 4) will appear larger in diameter than a stone that is cut thick (heavy). Conversely, a thick stone will appear smaller in diameter.

Furthermore, if the diamond has a thick girdle (see Chapter 4), the stone will appear smaller in diameter. If this girdle is faceted, it tends to hide the ugly, frosted look of a thick girdle, but the fact remains that the girdle is thick, and the stone suffers because it will appear smaller in diameter than one would expect at a given carat weight. These stones are therefore somewhat cheaper per carat.

8

How to Spot
a Fraud

How can you tell if a stone is really a diamond? As we have said many times, unless you are an expert—or see one—you cannot be sure about the identification of a stone. Nevertheless, there are a few simple tests you can perform that will show up most diamond frauds quite quickly. Here are a few things to look for.

Can you see a dark area when examining the stone? When you view properly, there will be no apparent dark spot within a diamond. With any other colorless stone, except strontium titanate or a foil-backed stone, there *will* be a dark spot. In the new synthetic, cubic zirconia (CZ), a dark spot can be observed when examined *very* carefully, but it is much more difficult to see than with other diamond substitutes.

Is news print readable or observable through the stone? If the stone is a round stone and is loose, or mounted in such a way as to allow you to place it table-down over some small news print, check whether you can see or read any portion of the lettering. If so, it is not a diamond.

Is the stone glued into the setting? Diamonds are *seldom* glued in. Rhinestones often are.

If a ring, is the back open or closed? If the stone is a properly set diamond, the back of the ring box or setting will always be open, allowing a portion of the pavilion to be readily observable. (Some very small rose-cut diamonds or *chips,* as seen in some antique jewelry, may be mounted with a closed back.) If a ring has a closed back, it is probably rhinestone, in which case the back is often closed in order to conceal the foil that has been applied to the back of the rhinestone.

Recently a young woman called and asked if we would examine an antique diamond ring she'd inherited from her great-grandmother. She mentioned that as she was cleaning it, one of its two diamonds had fallen out of the setting, and inside the setting she saw what she described as pieces of "mirror." She added, "Isn't that strange?" Of course my suspicions were immediately aroused, and upon examination of the piece, they were completely confirmed.

When we saw the piece, we could immediately understand why she felt this ring was a fine heirloom. The ring was beautiful. Its design was classic. It held two "diamonds" appearing to be approximately 1 carat each. The ring mounting was beautiful, finely worked filigree platinum. But the design of the mounting, which had been common in her great-grandmother's day, made viewing the stones from the side of the ring almost impossible. One could see the top of the stone, and the beautiful platinum work, but little more. Furthermore, the back was almost completely enclosed, except for a small round hole at the back of the setting (which would have led one to assume the stones were the real thing, since it wasn't completely closed, as was the case with most imitations at that time). The "set" diamond appeared to be a well-proportioned "old mine" cut (the cut of that day) with very good color. The loose stone, however, with some of the "shiny stuff" still clinging to it, lacked brilliance and fire.

This was one of the finest examples of fraud we had seen in a long time. The "stones" were well cut and proportioned; the mounting was beautifully worked in a precious metal; the stones were held by very small prongs, which was typical of good design at that time. But inside the mounting, backing the stones, was silver foil.

The use of silver foil is an effective method to "create" a diamond. It acts as a mirror to reflect light so that the stone appears so brilliant and lively that it can pass as a diamond. The foiling seen today consists of making the back facets into true mirrors and then giving the backs of these mirrors a protective coating of gilt paint. These are then set in jewelry so that their backs are hidden.

It's a sad story, but not an altogether uncommon one. We don't know how many more rings as cleverly done exist today, but approximately 5 percent of the antique jewelry we see is set with fake gems. Fine glass imitations (often referred to as *paste*) have been with us since the Venetians of Renaissance time perfected the art of glass-making—and fraud since time immemorial. Don't allow yourself to be deluded into believing that something you possess is "genuine" simply because it is "antique" or has "been in the family" for a long time.

Count the facets visible on the top. In cheaper glass imitations there are usually only 9 visible top facets, as opposed to 33 visible top facets in a diamond or "good" simulation. However, some small diamonds, such as those seen in side stones in some rings and some wedding bands, do show only 9 facets on top (referred to in the trade as *single cut* rather than brilliant cut). Of course, such diamonds are set in open-back mountings, whereas rhinestones would usually be set in closed-back mountings.

Examine the girdle of the stone. Most diamonds have a frosted appearance (unpolished having a ground-glass-like appearance). There are some diamond imitations that also have a frosted appearance, but of all of these, a diamond has the whitest "frostiness"—like clean, dry ground glass. (Note, however, that some diamonds do have polished or faceted girdles, and so this frostiness will not be observed.) You can develop an eye for this by asking a reliable jeweler to point out the differences between a polished girdle, an unpolished girdle, and a faceted girdle.

Check the symmetry of the cut. Since diamond is so valuable and symmetry so important to its overall appearance and desirability, the symmetry of the faceting on a diamond will be very carefully executed, whereas in diamond simulations the symmetry of the facets

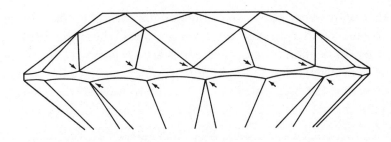

Misalignment of crown and pavilion

may be sloppy. For example, the eight kite-shaped facets (sometimes called bezel facets) will often be missing one or more points on the side, or on the top or bottom, showing a small straight edge rather than a point. This sloppy faceting can be an important indication that the stone in question is not a diamond, since it indicates that proper care was not taken (but some poorer-grade diamonds or old-cut diamonds may also show this sloppiness).

Are the crown and the pavilion of the stone properly aligned? While occasionally a diamond may show partial misalignment, imitations are frequently and often badly misaligned.

Are the facet edges or faces scratched, chipped, or worn? Diamond imitations include some stones that are very soft and/or brittle, such as zircon, GGG (a man-made simulation), Fabulite (a man-made diamond simulation also known as Wellington Diamond), and glass. Due to their lack of hardness and, in the case of zircon, possible brittleness, these imitations will show wear easily, and one can often detect scratches or chips on the facet edges or faces. The edges are somewhat more vulnerable and scratches or chips may be more easily seen there, so check the edges first. Then check the flat faces for scratches. Check the areas that would be most exposed, as well as around the prongs (where a setter might accidentally have scratched the stone while setting it).

Zircon, which is not particularly soft, is very brittle, and it will almost always show chipping at the edges of the facets if the stone has been worn in jewelry for any length of time (a year or more). Glass and Fabulite will also show scratches after minimal exposure to handling and wear. (Fabulite also differs from diamond in its fire—it will show even *more* fire than diamond, but with a strong bluishness to it.)

Also, with a very good eye or the aid of a magnifier, one can notice an absence of sharpness to the lines or edges where the facets come together. In diamond these facet edges are very sharp because of the stone's spectacular hardness. In most simulation, since the stone is so much softer, the final polishing technique rounds off these edges.

Some diamond look-alikes, however, are more durable and resistant to noticeable wear. These include colorless synthetic spinel, colorless synthetic sapphire, colorless quartz, YAG (man-made), and CZ (cubic zirconia, also man-made). While these may scratch or chip over time with regular wear and daily abuse, scratches or chips will probably not be easily observed. These stones, however, can be distinguished from diamond simply by examining as already described.

Examine the stone, loose or mounted, for fluorescence under ultraviolet light. We do not feel this is something readily accomplished by an amateur, nor comprehensible to the average person because of the numerous variables and scientific complexities. If, after the above tests, you still have doubt, take the stone to a qualified gemologist with lab facilities and ask him to identify the stone. If it is a diamond, have him note the nature of the stone's fluorescence, as it can prove a valuable tool for identification if ever needed.

An Important Word About CZ

CZ is the best diamond simulation made to date, and even some jewelers have taken them for diamonds.

Shortly after the appearance of CZ, several well-known Washington, D.C., jewelers found themselves stuck with CZ instead of their nice 1-carat diamonds. The crooks were very clever. A well-dressed couple would arrive at the diamond counter and ask to see various 1-carat, round, brilliant-cut loose diamonds. Because of their fine appearance and educated manner, the jeweler's guard was relaxed. The couple would then leave, not making a purchase decision just then, but promising to return. When the jeweler went to replace his merchandise, "something" didn't seem quite right. Upon close examination, the jeweler discovered that the "nice couple" had pocketed the genuine diamonds and substituted CZ.

CZ is almost as brilliant as diamond, has even greater fire (which masks its lesser brilliance), and is relatively hard, giving it good durability and wearability. CZ is also being produced today in fancy colors—red, green, and yellow—and CZ can provide a nice diamond "alternative" as a means to offset or dress up colored semiprecious stones in jewelry if diamonds are unaffordable.

But make sure you *know* what you are buying. For example, if you are shown a lovely amethyst or sapphire ring dressed up with "diamonds," make sure to ask whether the colorless stones are diamonds. And if you are having your own piece of jewelry custom made, you might want to consider using CZ. You can ask your jeweler to order them for you. Also, they make stunning stud earrings and other jewelry that can be worn every day . . . and you need not worry if they are stolen—your real gems can be safe in your vault!

How Can You Tell If You Have a CZ?

Some of the tests already discussed may help you detect a CZ. The following, however, may eliminate any remaining doubt.

If it is a loose stone, have it weighed. CZ is much heavier than a diamond of similar size. If you are familiar with diamond sizes (see pages 50 and 51) or have a spread gauge (which can be purchased for under $5), you can estimate the diamond carat weight by its spread. The loose stone can be weighed on a scale, which most jewelers have handy, and you can determine how much it should weigh if a diamond. If the weight is *much* greater than the diamond weight should be, based on its spread, then it is *not* a diamond. A CZ is approximately 75 percent heavier than a diamond of the same spread. For example, a 1-carat (diamond spread) CZ weighs 1¾ carats; a ²⁵⁄₁₀₀ carat (diamond spread) CZ weighs approximately ⁴⁰⁄₁₀₀ carat.

Look at the girdle. If it is frosted, unlike diamond, it will have a subdued whiteness resembling slightly wet or oiled frosted glass. Unfortunately, one must have some experience looking at girdles in order to differentiate between the appearance of frosted CZ and frosted diamond girdles.

Test the stone with a carbide scriber. CZ can be scratched with a fine-point carbide scriber, also available at most jewelry supply houses for under $10. If the scriber is forcibly pushed perpendicularly to any of the facets (the table being the easiest) and then drawn across this flat surface, you will scratch it. You cannot scratch a diamond except with another diamond. But be sensible . . . and considerate. Don't heedlessly scratch merchandise that doesn't belong to you—particularly if the jeweler or seller doesn't represent the stone as diamond.

Examine the stone, loose or mounted, for fluorescence. Both CZ and diamond fluoresce, but the colors and intensities will be different.

If after the tests you have some questions, take the stone to a qualified gemologist with lab facilities and ask him to identify it.

Types of Misrepresentation

There are five areas in which diamond fraud or misrepresentation usually occur. The consumer should be sensitive to:

1. Weight misrepresentation
2. Color alteration and misgrading

COMPARISON OF DIAMOND AND DIAMOND LOOK-ALIKES

NAME OF STONE	HARDNESS (MOHS' SCALE 1-10) 1 = SOFT, 10 = HARDEST	READ-THROUGH*	DEGREE OF DISPERSION (FIRE, FLASHES OF COLOR OBSERVED)	WEARABILITY
Diamond	10 (Hardest natural substance in existence)	None, if properly cut	High; lots of fire and liveliness	Excellent
Strontium titanate (also known as "Fabulite" or "Wellington Diamond")	5-6 (Soft)	None, if properly cut	Extremely high; too high (much more than diamond); shows lots of blue flashes	Poor—scratches and wears badly
Synthetic cubic zirconia (CZ)	8.5 (Hard)	Slight	Very high; lots of life	Very good
Gadolinium gallium garnet (GGG; produced very briefly)	6.5 (Somewhat soft)	Moderate	High; almost identical to diamond	Fair—scratches easily; wears badly; sunlight causes brownish discoloration
Yttrium aluminum garnet (YAG; used extensively)	8.5 (Hard)	Strong	Very low; almost no visible display of fire	Good
Synthetic rutile (shows yellowish color)	6.5 (Soft)	None	Extremely high; lots of life—but strong yellowish flashes	Poor; scratches easily and shows excessive wear
Zircon	7.5 (Moderately hard)	Moderate	Good; lively	Fair—hard but brittle, so chips easily and shows wear equivalent to much softer stones
Synthetic sapphire	9 (Very hard)	Very strong	Very low; little life or display of color flashes	Very good
Synthetic spinel	8 (Hard)	Very strong	Low; little "life"	Very good
Glass	5-6.5 (Soft)	Very strong	Variable—low to good depending on quality of glass and cut	Poor; susceptible to scratches, chipping, and excessive wear

*This technique—the ability and ease with which one can read print while looking through the stone—is meaningful only when looking at round, brilliant-cut stones (although it is *sometimes* observable in ovals and some fancy cuts).

DIAMOND AND DIAMOND LOOK-ALIKES:
CARAT WEIGHT/SIZE DIFFERENCES

Stone	Specific Gravity	.50 ct	1 ct	1.50 ct	2 ct
Diamond	S.G.—3.52	5.2 mm	6.5 mm	7.4 mm	8.2 mm
Synthetic Rutile	S.G.—4.25	4.9 mm	6.1 mm	7.0 mm	7.7 mm
Strontium Titanate	S.G.—5.13	4.6 mm	5.8 mm	6.6 mm	7.3 mm
Synthetic Cubic Zirconia	S.G.—5.67	4.4 mm	5.5 mm	6.3 mm	7.0 mm
GGG	S.G.—7.05	4.1 mm	5.1 mm	5.9 mm	6.5 mm
Zircon	S.G.—4.69	4.7 mm	5.9 mm	6.8 mm	7.5 mm
YAG	S.G.—4.55	4.7 mm	6.0 mm	6.8 mm	7.5 mm
Synthetic Sapphire	S.G.—3.99	4.9 mm	6.2 mm	7.1 mm	7.8 mm
Synthetic Spinel	S.G.—3.63	5.1 mm	6.4 mm	7.3 mm	8.1 mm

This chart illustrates how density affects the size of diamonds and various look-alikes. The chart is based on identically cut, standard round brilliant-cut stones. (S.G. means specific gravity, the density of the substance.)

3. Flaw concealment and misgrading
4. Certification—alteration and counterfeit production
5. Come-on and flamboyant advertising (Chapter 9)

Weight

Giving "total weight" where more than one stone is involved, rather than the exact weight of the main stone, is misrepresenting. Sometimes a customer buying a diamond ring with side stones, when asking about the "size" of the diamond, is given a diamond weight that actually represents the total weight of all the stones but is presented in such a way that the customer believes it to be the weight of the main, central stone. This is in strict violation of FTC rulings. In giving the weight, particularly on any display card, descriptive tag, or other type of advertising for a particular piece of jewelry, the weight of the main stone(s) should be clearly indicated, and the total weight of all the stones should also be indicated.

Thus, if you purchase a "3-carat diamond" ring with three stones—one large center stone and two small side stones (as found in many engagement rings)—the center stone's weight should be clearly stated; for example, "The weight of the center stone is 2.80 carats, with 2 side stones that weigh .10 carat each, for a total weight of 3 carats."

There is a tremendous price difference between a single stone weighing 3 carats and numerous stones having a total weight of 3 carats. A single 3-carat stone could sell for $100,000, while 3 carats consisting of numerous stones (even with some weighing as much as a carat or more) of good quality could sell anywhere from $5,000 to $10,000, depending upon how many and what quality.

Use of the Word Spread in Response to Questions About Weight or Size

A consumer inquiring about the weight of a diamond usually asks the wrong question, as discussed earlier, due to confusion between size and weight. Usually the jeweler will be asked how large the stone is, rather than how much it weighs. In any case, the answer should provide the *exact carat weight*. Where the response includes the word *spread* ("This stone has an *x*-carat spread" or "This stone spreads *x* carats"), *beware*. A stone that spreads 1 carat is not the same thing as a stone that weighs 1 carat. It simply means it *looks like* a 1-carat stone in its width (or width and length if a fancy-cut diamond).

In diamond-trade language a spread stone is one with thin propor-tions—it's somewhat "pancaked." The cut and proportion may be poor, and the stone will therefore lack life and should sell for less per carat than a well-cut stone. If you see a diamond that looks like it is about 1 carat, and the price seems particularly attractive, make sure you ask what the *exact actual weight* is. Look at the stone carefully, fo-cusing your attention on its brilliance and fire, and ask yourself if it's really pretty and lively, and whether you really like it.

A fine 1-carat stone will cost much more per carat than a stone that is only .90 carat, for example, but seems as large because of its spread.

To illustrate our point even more clearly in terms of dollar value, a first-quality diamond weighing *from 1 full carat to 1.06 carats has a cost per carat approximately 45 percent more than a .94 carat that spreads 1 carat.* (Some "slightly spread" stones are still very pretty and lively, but their price should be 15 to 25 percent less than other stones *of the same size.*)

Illusion Mounting

This refers to mounting a stone in a setting that creates the illusion that the stone is larger than it actually is. This in and of itself may not be misleading, or in any way fraudulent. In fact, it may be preferable

An illusion setting

to the customer. But don't be misled as to the size of a stone mounted in this manner. Make sure you *know* what you are getting.

Color

Methods of Enhancing Color Artificially

Touching the culet, or side, of a slightly yellow stone with a coating of purple ink such as is found in an indelible pencil. The purple neutralizes the yellow, producing a whiter-looking stone. This can be easily detected by washing the stone in alcohol or water.

If you have any questions about the color, tactfully request that the stone be washed (in front of you) for "better examination." A reputable jeweler should have no objection to this request.

Improving the color by utilizing a sputtering technique. This involves sputtering a very thin coating of a special substance over the stone or part of the stone (usually the back, where it will be harder to detect when mounted). This substance again neutralizes the yellow and thereby improves the color. This technique is not frequently used, but stones treated in this manner do appear often enough to be worth mentioning.

It does *not* wash off. It can be removed in two ways: by rubbing the stone briskly and firmly with a cleanser or by boiling the stone carefully in sulfuric acid.

If the stone is already mounted and is coated on the back, using cleanser is not feasible. The sulfuric acid method is the only way. But please note, it is *extremely dangerous*, and must be conducted by an experienced person. We cannot understate the hazards of conducting this test.

Coating the diamond with chemicals and baking it in a small lab-type furnace. This technique also tends to neutralize some of the yellow, thereby producing a better color grade. This coating will be removed eventually by repeated hot ultrasonic cleanings, during which the coating will be gradually eroded. A more rapid removal can be accomplished by the more dangerous method of boiling in sulfuric acid.

Radiation treatment. Exposing off-colored diamonds, such as yellowish- or brownish-tinted stones, and also badly flawed stones, to certain types of radiation can result in the production of fancy colored stones—canary yellow, greens, blues, or pinks.

This treatment greatly enhances their salability because these fancy colors are very desirable. In and of itself, radiation is not fraud; in fact, it may enable one otherwise unable to afford a fancy to be able to afford one. But again, just be sure it is properly represented and you *know* what you are buying, and that you are buying it at the right price—which is much lower than that of the natural fancy.

Treated stones must be represented as "treated stones" and should be priced accordingly. Unfortunately, too often, in passing through many hands, the fact that they have been "treated" or "radiated" or "bombarded" is overlooked or forgotten—intentionally or accidentally.

Whether the color is natural or treated can be determined by spectroscopic examination, which can be provided by a highly skilled gemologist. Not many gemologists, however, are competent with spectroscopic procedures, and it may be time-consuming. If you wish to verify a fancy stone as natural, ask the gemologist if he is experienced in conducting such testing. If he is not, he may be able to recommend someone who is.

Mountings

Sometimes the mounting can slightly enhance color. Again, when possible, it is preferable to examine the stone unmounted.

Erroneous Color Grading

This may be deliberate, or it may be the result of the jeweler's limited knowledge. One is safer considering the purchase of a stone that has had important data, such as color, "certificated" by one of several different laboratories now offering this service. Many jewelry firms and investment houses now offer "certificated" stones. They usually sell for slightly more per carat, but provide an element of security for the average consumer, as well as credible documentation if one wishes to sell this stone at some future time.

Flaw Concealment

Where possible, flaws are concealed by their settings. The good stone setter will try to set a stone in such a manner that the prong (or prongs) will help to conceal any visible flaws. This is one reason flaws near or at the girdle will downgrade a stone less than those found in the center of a stone. Aside from the fact that they are simply less visible here, they may also become "invisible" when the stone is set.

Similarly, flaws can be concealed under the bezel in a bezel-set stone. A bezel setting is a rim of metal that encases the girdle, as in a pair of eyeglasses; the rim of metal holding the lens could be called a bezel setting. While this type of setting hasn't been seen much in diamond jewelry in the past, we are beginning to see more and more bezel settings in diamond jewelry because it can protect the girdle, and can accent an unusual shape very nicely. And, of course, this too can conceal in the same manner as prong settings. However, note that the bezel setting also prevents examination of the girdle. This makes examination for naturals, small chips, slight repairs, and the girdle thickness itself impossible unless the stone is removed from the setting.

Is Concealment Fraud or Misrepresentation?

There is nothing fraudulent in this as long as the stone is properly represented. The only danger is that not only may the customer not see it but the jeweler may not have seen it.

We know of situations where a jeweler purchases mounted goods from a dealer at a fair price, thinking he is getting an unusually good price because he can't spot the flaw. He then does one of two things—sells the ring at his normal markup, giving the buyer a fair price for the ring, but possibly representing it as a finer quality and therefore a better value for the price than it really is . . . unknowingly. Or he may take advantage of an opportunity here to make a higher profit, and mark the ring up to what he feels would be a fair price, when in fact it is now overpriced . . . again, unknowingly.

Can Concealment Affect Value?

In most diamonds other than FL or IF, the presence of a minor flaw concealed under a prong will not affect the price significantly. However, a diamond represented as FL or IF may have a small blemish or inclusion hidden under a prong, which should have been classified as IF or VVS_1. The difference here may represent a very large price difference on larger stones with fine body color.

Certification of Diamonds

In the United States today, most fine diamonds of 1 carat or larger have been *certificated* prior to being set by one of the well-known gem labs (GIA and IGL—see page 193). This means that the stone will not only have been certified as genuine, but will have an accompanying *certificate* that will *fully* describe it, providing all the important information such as color grade, flaw grade, weight, cut/proportion, etc. If one is considering the purchase of a very fine diamond weighing 1 carat or more, which has not been certificated, we would strongly recommend that the stone be certificated prior to purchase (even if this means having a stone that is already set removed from the setting—no reputable lab will certificate a mounted diamond—and reset). Given the significant difference in cost that can result from a grading error in these rarer grades, we believe it is worth any inconvenience.

Unfortunately, the confidence of the public in certificated stones has given rise to the practice of altering and counterfeiting certificates. While you can be relatively sure that certificated stones sold by reputable, established jewelry firms are exactly what they claim to be, there are some suppliers and dealers who are seizing opportunities to prey upon the unsuspecting.

Altering Certificates

This involves changing information on an otherwise valid certificate—changing the flaw or color grade stated. If you have any question regarding information on the certificate, a phone call to the lab giving them the certificate number and date will enable you to verify the information on your certificate.

Counterfeit Certificates

This practice is outright fraud and consists of several techniques:

- Producing a "GIA" (or other equally credible lab) certificate that is not in fact a GIA certificate. An astute appraiser may detect the difference in the seal on the certificate. Again, if you have any reason to be suspicious, a call to the lab in question will usually expose this fraud.
- Producing a certificate from a nonexistent lab. This is becoming an increasing problem today. Stones accompanied by fancy "certificates" from impressive sounding labs that don't exist are appearing more and more frequently. GIA and IGL are presently the most widely recognized certificating labs. This doesn't mean that a less well-known gemologist can't certificate a stone for a customer, which would certainly accompany the piece should it be sold. However, if it is not from one of the recog-

nized labs it should be carefully checked. Have jewelers in the area heard of this lab? Has the Better Business Bureau had any complaints. If the lab seems legitimate, call to verify the information on the certificate, and if all seems in order, you can probably rest comfortably.

Switching the Stone Described on a Certificate

In this situation the certificate is bona fide but the stone has been switched. To protect both the consumer and the certificating lab, some labs today are taking advantage of ingenious techniques to ensure against switching, by permanently marking the stone in some way. For example, GIA can now actually inscribe the certificate number which is visible only under magnification, directly onto the diamond itself, along the girdle. By so doing, one can very easily be sure a specific stone matches a specific certificate simply by matching the numbers. There is an additional fee for this service.

In the absence of such a mark, one clue to a switched stone might be provided by the carat weight and the dimensions given on the certificate. If the measurements match exactly, the probability is slim that the stone has been switched (provided the certificate hasn't been altered). Again, a phone call can verify such information. If the measurements don't match, you know there is a mistake somewhere that warrants immediate investigation. If the measurements do match, then all the specifications provided on the certificate—fluorescence, depth percentage, table spread, crown angles, symmetry, color, clarity—should be checked to see if the stone and the certificate match.

Unfortunately, if the stone has been mounted it may be difficult to get precise measurements to compare. In this case, if there is any cause for suspicion, the consumer has little recourse unless the seller allows the consumer to have the certificate and stone verified by a qualified gemologist appraiser (removing the stone from the setting). This arrangement requires an understanding *in writing* that the stone can be returned within a certain time limit if the customer learns of misrepresentation.

Always make sure in this situation, for both your protection and the jeweler's, that the jeweler writes down on the bill of sale or memo all of the stone's dimensions as best as he can determine—diameter or length and widths, depth percentage, and weight. This is to ensure that you aren't accused of switching the stone after leaving the premises, in the event you must return the stone.

The jeweler may not allow this verification—and some won't, simply because they've been victims themselves or it isn't worth the inconvenience to them. In this case, you might ask the jeweler if he would get the stone certificated by one of the recognized labs (GIA, IGI). Many jewelers today are happy to provide this service for you. If not, then you must decide how badly you want the stone, how much you feel you can trust the jeweler, and what degree of monetary risk you can afford.

We would personally never purchase, at any price, a certificated diamond sold in a sealed container because there is no way to take the stone out to verify the data on the certificate. Unfortunately, there is a need to seal the diamonds to prevent switching in mail-order operations, and we do not wish to suggest that these stones are not as represented. But the possibility exists, and the consumer is usually left with no recourse should it be learned later that the certificate incorrectly graded the stone. Once the seal is broken, you have no way to prove that the stone in question was the one originally sealed in the package. Also, since the diamond may be put in a vault or safe deposit box, it could be years before the possible deception or error is detected.

If you have, or wish to purchase, such a stone, we recommend that you formally arrange with the seller terms under which the seal may be broken so that an independent gemologist/appraiser can verify the stone's specifications, with the buyer retaining the right to return the gem if it is found not to be as represented.

A Word About Protecting Your Diamonds with Gemprint

Advanced techniques have provided us with an important new service that can positively identify any diamond, and may play an increasing role in reducing theft and accidental loss. This service is called Gemprint.

Gemprint provides a means of identifying any diamond, even stones already mounted in settings, by taking a photograph of the pattern of reflections created when a low-level laser beam hits the gem. Each diamond produces a unique pattern, which is documented on photographic film and, as with fingerprints, no two are ever alike.

One could describe Gemprint as a diamond's "fingerprint."

The process takes only a few minutes. For a nominal cost ($35 to $50), two photographs are taken. One is given to the customer, accompanied by a numbered certificate of registration. The second is filed in the Gemprint Central Registry in Chicago. Gemprint sends the owner a confirmation of the registration, and a "notice of loss" form to hold for any future need.

If the stone is ever lost or stolen, the owner sends the notice-of-loss form to Gemprint, which immediately notifies the police. The police can then verify the identification of recovered lost or stolen diamonds with the registry, so that the stone can be returned to its rightful owner.

As another safeguard, Gemprint also checks each new registration against its lost-and-stolen file before confirming and storing the registration. Gemprint can also be useful in situations where a diamond, or diamond jewelry, has been left for repair, cleaning, or resetting, to assure the owner that he has gotten back his own stone.

Some insurance companies today give an annual 10 percent off the premium paid on a floater policy insuring a diamond that has been Gemprinted. Check with your insurance company.

Gemprint is available in about 650 locations in the U.S. (jewelry stores, gem labs, dealers). You can obtain the name of the location nearest you by contacting Gemprint directly: Gemprint, Ltd., 1901 N. Naper Blvd., Naperville, IL 60540 (312)505-1161.

9

Bait or Flamboyant Advertising

We've all seen come-on or misrepresentative advertising. Quite simply, it is advertising that lures the buyer into a store or into making a purchase. This is seen frequently today in the mail-order business. The Better Business Bureau, in their booklet *Facts You Should Know About Jewelry*, describes these practices very well. (This booklet is available upon request.) Some of the practices they describe are:

Bait advertising. Articles are advertised at bargain prices, but the seller has no intention of selling them. When you arrive, the article they advertised is "sold out," but they have something else, which, of course, costs more. Often, too, goods are of inferior quality.

Buying "wholesale." In this case the seller claims to be selling products at wholesale prices, when in fact they are selling merely at a discount. Few firms sell truly at wholesale.

Catalog scheme. The seller issues a catalog with fictitious wholesale or discounted items.

Deposit scheme. The seller asks the customer for a deposit, which will be returned if the buyer is dissatisfied. In reality, the seller will only provide credit toward the purchase of other goods.

Factory-gate scheme. The manufacturer induces the workers to take merchandise such as watches or other jewelry "on approval" simply by signing a receipt. The receipt turns out to be a binding contract to pay for the merchandise.

Fictitious allowances. These occur with trade-ins. The seller jacks up

73

the price of the item you are buying to cover the trade-in allowance.

Fictitious comparative prices. This is advertising with two prices, an "original" price and a "sale" price. The "original" price is fictitious, or much higher than the item is worth.

Fictitious list prices. The list price for the item is much higher than the sale price—but, of course, the list price is not true.

Fictitious preticketing. The seller attaches a price tag showing a high fictitious price on "reduced" merchandise.

These methods are used in the selling of gems and jewelry, just as they are for selling automobiles, clothing, food, or any other commodity. Beware of them. Learn to judge for yourself the value of the gems and the current selling prices, and trust your judgment.

Come-on Ads

In recent years many ads have been circulated offering diamonds, rubies, or emeralds for unbelievable prices such as $10 for a pair of diamond earrings or $19.95 for a diamond ring. These ads are just one more new and more sophisticated form of deception. The next time you see one, study it carefully and take note of the various tactics used to deceive the buyer.

The ads often appear in respected publications. This, in itself, lends credibility. Often the seller offers a money-back guarantee to further lure the buyer into believing this must be safe. Often the seller claims the stone is "genuine." Because of truth-in-advertising laws, the buyer believes that the goods must be genuine if the advertiser claims they are. Usually the seller offers a certificate that provides even further assurance.

In fact, the buyer will receive precisely what was advertised. The stones will be genuine and of the size advertised. Also, the money-back guarantee and the certificate usually prove to be true and valid. However, you must read between the lines. With a closer look, the facts reveal less than you would expect.

Size. Often the ads will offer ¼ carat total weight for rubies, sapphires, or emeralds and .25 point for diamonds. This means that each earring or ring consisting of rubies, sapphires, or emeralds has stones that weigh ⅛ carat; moreover, the ⅛ carat may consist of several small stones or chips, not one ⅛-carat stone.

The diamond size is extremely deceptive. A .25-point stone is *not* ¼ carat, as one might expect. One-quarter carat is 25 points (note the placement of the decimal point); there are 100 points in a carat. With the diamond, you would be receiving ¹⁄₄₀₀ of 1 carat, not ¼ carat. (This is even more deceptive, since other gems in the ad are ¼ carat.) In any case, the diamond offered is extremely small, probably the size of a fleck of dandruff.

Genuineness. The stones one receives from this type of advertisement are genuine. However, there is no description of color, flaw grade, or cut. One expects to receive a lovely stone—a beautiful, sparkling diamond, a transparent, lively emerald, ruby, or sapphire.

The buyer receives flawed, badly cut diamonds and cloudy, flawed, unattractive colored gems. In other words, the buyer receives exactly what he paid for. Moreover, the stones will have *no resale value* whatsoever.

The money-back guarantee and the certificate. Again, in point of fact, these promises are true. However, given the small price paid, would it be worth the trouble to return the goods for a refund? Also, what guarantee is there that the supplier will still be in business or located at the same address by the time you receive your jewelry and return it?

With regard to "certification," certificated by whom? Is this specified? And even if you doubt the certification, would you bother spending $25 or more to have a gemologist appraise the jewelry or verify the certificate?

These are just a few of the deceptions buried in these schemes. As we have said, everything printed in these advertisements is true, but is the jewelry of sufficient value to warrant buying it at all? Examine each ad very carefully, apply what you now know, and you should be able to see through most of them.

And remember: No one gives away a valuable gem. There are very few "steals," and even fewer people qualified to truly know a "steal" when they see one.

Always deal with reputable jewelers with established reputations. Don't be afraid to ask questions.

10

What to Ask When Buying a Diamond

You should always ask the following questions before purchasing a fine diamond of 1-carat size or larger. Most jewelers don't take the time to grade smaller stones, although .50- and .75-carat stones are now beginning to appear with certificates verifying color and flaw grades. An experienced jeweler should be able to provide this information for stones .50 carats and up, or offer to find out for you.

These are the questions you should ask:

1. What is the exact carat weight? (Be sure its weight is given, not its spread.)
2. What is its color grade? (and what grading system was used?)
3. What is its clarity (flaw) grade? (Again, ask what system was used.)
4. How is it cut? (marquise, brilliant, emerald?)
5. What are the exact millimeter dimensions of the stone?
6. Is this stone certificated?

These questions are basic. Be sure to find out what system was used to grade the stone's color and clarity, such as GIA or IGL.

Be sure to get the exact millimeter dimensions of the stone. (The dimensions can be approximated if the stone is mounted.) Make sure you are given the girdle diameter; if the stone is not uniformly round, get two girdle diameters. Also, get the dimension from the table to the

77

culet and the depth percentage. With fancy cuts (except for triangular-shaped diamonds) ask for the length and width dimensions.

Be especially careful if the diamond is being taken out on consignment, on a jeweler's memorandum or sales slip, or on a contingency sale. Having the measurements on a jeweler's memorandum helps protect you from being accused of switching should you have to return the stone for any reason.

Always ask if the stone is certificated, and, if so, make sure that the certificate accompanies the stone. If you are unable to obtain the certificate or a copy, find out who determined the color and flaw grades, and make sure that the sale is contingent upon the stone's having the grades represented by the salesperson.

Additional Questions

Does This Stone Have a Good Make?

What are the proportions of this stone? How do its proportions compare to the ideal stone? Remember, much variance can exist and a stone can still be a beautiful, desirable gem even if it does not conform to the "ideal." If you have any question about the stone's brilliance and liveliness, you should ask specifically about the proportioning of the cut.

Does This Stone Show Any Fluorescence?

If a diamond fluoresces blue when viewed in daylight or under daylight-type fluorescent light, it will appear to have better color than it actually has. This can be a desirable quality so long as the stone has not been graded or classified as having finer color than it has. A diamond may also fluoresce yellow, which means that in a certain light its color could appear worse than it actually is. If the stone has been certificated, any fluorescence should be indicated on the certificate. If it has not been certificated, the jeweler may not know its true color.

Special Tips When Buying a Diamond

Ask the Jeweler to Clean the Stone

Don't hesitate to ask to have the stone cleaned before you examine it. Cleaning will remove dirt, grease, or indelible purple ink. Cleaning is best done in an ultrasonic cleaner.

View the Stone Against a Dead White Background

When looking at unmounted stones, look at them only against a dead-white background such as white blotter paper or a white business card, or on a grading trough. (See page 34.) Look at the stone against the white background so that you are looking at it through the side, not down through the table. Tilt the stone toward a good light source (daylight fluorescent lamp is best). If the stone shows any yellow body tint when viewed through the girdle, if the stone is not as colorless as an ice cube, then the diamond is off-color.

Get the Facts on a Bill of Sale

Ask that all the facts concerning the stone be put on the bill of sale. These include the carat weight, the color and flaw grades, the cut, the dimensions. Also, be sure you obtain the certificate on any certificated stone.

Verify Facts with a Gemologist

If a stone is 1 carat or larger *and not certificated,* make the sale contingent upon verification of the facts by a qualified gemologist, gem-testing lab, or GIA. (GIA will not estimate dollar value, but they will verify color, flaw grade, make, fluorescence, weight, and other factual matters.)

Weigh the Facts

Color is the most important consideration when buying a diamond. If the color is good, then consider flaw grade, cut, and proportion (make), in that order. The following charts provide an idea of the *effect of color relative to the flaw grade* on the *retail* dollar value of the stone. Note the tremendous price fluctuation among stones of the same size due to differences in flaw grades and color grades, and the disproportionate jumps in cost per carat depending upon size.

To Sum Up

You are now well informed about diamonds and how to buy them. Use your information, but remember, it takes years of formal training and experience to become a true expert. Also, given an intelligent and informed viewing of the stone, if you find it lively, beautiful, and affordable, it is probably a good purchase for you.

HOW VARIABLES OF COLOR AND FLAW GRADE AFFECT DIAMOND PRICING

Diamond Price Guide, July1987—prices quoted are *per carat*
(Using GIA scale for comparison)

⅓-Carat Round Brilliant (.30+)

Flaw (Clarity) Grade

		IF	VVS$_1$	VVS$_2$	VS$_1$	VS$_2$	SI$_1$	SI$_2$	I$_1$	
	D	6,900	6,300	6,000	5,700	5,200	4,200	3,900	3,300	D
	E	6,300	6,000	5,700	5,400	4,800	3,900	3,600	3,000	E
	F	6,000	5,700	5,400	5,100	4,500	3,600	3,300	2,700	F
Color Grade	G	5,700	5,400	5,100	4,800	4,200	3,300	3,000	2,500	G
	H	5,100	4,800	4,200	3,900	3,600	3,000	2,700	2,400	H
	I	4,200	3,900	3,600	3,300	3,000	2,700	2,400	2,000	I
	J	3,900	3,600	3,300	3,000	2,700	2,400	2,100	1,800	J
	K	3,600	3,200	2,700	2,600	2,400	2,100	1,800	1,500	K
		IF	VVS$_1$	VVS$_2$	VS$_1$	VS$_2$	SI$_1$	SI$_2$	I$_1$	

Notice both the tremendous price fluctuation among stones of the same size due to differences in the flaw grades and color grades, and the disproportionate jumps in cost *per carat*, depending upon size.

80

HOW VARIABLES OF COLOR AND FLAW GRADE AFFECT DIAMOND PRICING

Diamond Price Guide, July1987—prices quoted are *per carat*
(Using GIA scale for comparison)

½-Carat Round Brilliant (.50+)

Flaw (Clarity) Grade

		IF	VVS$_1$	VVS$_2$	VS$_1$	VS$_2$	SI$_1$	SI$_2$	I$_1$	
	D	14,300	10,400	9,900	9,000	7,500	6,600	6,000	4,500	D
	E	10,400	9,900	9,300	8,400	7,200	6,300	5,700	4,200	E
	F	9,900	9,300	8,700	7,800	6,900	6,000	5,400	3,900	F
Color Grade	G	9,300	8,700	7,500	7,200	6,600	5,700	5,100	3,600	G
	H	8,700	7,500	6,900	6,600	6,300	5,400	4,800	3,300	H
	I	7,200	6,600	6,300	6,000	5,400	4,800	4,300	3,000	I
	J	6,000	5,400	5,100	4,900	4,600	4,200	3,600	2,700	J
	K	4,800	4,600	4,500	4,200	4,100	3,600	3,000	2,400	K
		IF	VVS$_1$	VVS$_2$	VS$_1$	VS$_2$	SI$_1$	SI$_2$	I$_1$	

Notice both the tremendous price fluctuation among stones of the same size due to differences in the flaw grades and color grades, and the disproportionate jumps in cost *per carat*, depending upon size.

81

HOW VARIABLES OF COLOR AND FLAW GRADE AFFECT DIAMOND PRICING

Diamond Price Guide, July1987—prices quoted are *per carat* (Using GIA scale for comparison)

¾-*Carat Round Brilliant* (.70+)

Flaw (Clarity) Grade

Color Grade	IF	VVS_1	VVS_2	VS_1	VS_2	SI_1	SI_2	I_1	
D	17,600	12,200	11,000	9,900	8,800	7,400	6,800	5,400	D
E	12,200	11,000	10,200	9,000	8,200	7,100	6,600	5,200	E
F	11,000	10,200	9,300	8,500	7,700	6,800	6,200	4,900	F
G	10,200	9,300	8,200	7,700	7,100	6,600	6,000	4,600	G
H	9,300	8,200	7,700	7,100	6,600	6,000	5,400	4,300	H
I	8,000	7,100	6,800	6,200	6,000	5,400	4,900	4,100	I
J	6,600	6,200	6,000	5,800	5,400	4,900	4,300	3,800	J
K	5,800	5,400	5,200	4,900	4,600	4,300	3,800	3,500	K
	IF	VVS_1	VVS_2	VS_1	VS_2	SI_1	SI_2	I_1	

Notice both the tremendous price fluctuation among stones of the same size due to differences in the flaw grades and color grades, and the disproportionate jumps in cost *per carat*, depending upon size.

HOW VARIABLES OF COLOR AND FLAW GRADE
AFFECT DIAMOND PRICING

Diamond Price Guide, July 1987—prices quoted are *per carat*
(Using GIA scale for comparison)

1-Carat Round Brilliant (1.00+)

Flaw (Clarity) Grade

	IF	VVS$_1$	VVS$_2$	VS$_1$	VS$_2$	SI$_1$	SI$_2$	I$_1$	
D	32,000	20,000	16,000	11,600	10,400	8,400	7,500	5,300	**D**
E	20,000	16,000	13,000	10,400	9,400	7,600	7,000	4,900	**E**
F	16,000	13,000	11,000	9,400	8,400	7,500	6,600	4,600	**F**
G	13,600	11,000	9,400	8,400	7,400	7,000	6,200	4,400	**G**
H	11,600	9,400	8,400	7,400	7,000	6,700	5,900	4,300	**H**
I	8,400	8,000	7,700	7,000	6,600	6,200	5,500	4,200	**I**
J	7,700	7,200	6,800	6,200	5,900	5,700	5,100	4,000	**J**
K	6,400	6,000	5,700	5,500	5,300	5,100	4,900	3,800	**K**
	IF	VVS$_1$	VVS$_2$	VS$_1$	VS$_2$	SI$_1$	SI$_2$	I$_1$	

Color Grade

Notice both the tremendous price fluctuation among stones of the same size due to differences in the flaw grades and color grades, and the disproportionate jumps in cost *per carat*, depending upon size.

83

HOW VARIABLES OF COLOR AND FLAW GRADE AFFECT DIAMOND PRICING

Diamond Price Guide, July1987—prices quoted are *per carat* (Using GIA scale for comparison)

2-Carat Round Brilliant (2.00+)

Flaw (Clarity) Grade

	IF	VVS$_1$	VVS$_2$	VS$_1$	VS$_2$	SI$_1$	SI$_2$	I$_1$	
D	39,000	26,000	22,400	16,800	14,000	11,800	9,400	6,800	**D**
E	27,000	22,000	19,400	15,800	13,400	11,400	9,000	6,400	**E**
F	23,000	19,000	16,400	14,400	12,800	10,800	8,600	6,000	**F**
G	20,000	16,400	14,400	13,400	11,400	9,600	8,200	5,600	**G**
H	17,000	14,400	13,400	11,400	10,400	8,800	7,600	5,400	**H**
I	12,000	10,400	10,000	9,400	8,400	7,600	6,800	5,200	**I**
J	10,000	9,400	9,000	8,200	7,600	6,800	6,200	4,800	**J**
K	9,000	8,000	7,600	7,200	6,800	6,000	5,600	4,400	**K**
	IF	VVS$_1$	VVS$_2$	VS$_1$	VS$_2$	SI$_1$	SI$_2$	I$_1$	

Color Grade (left vertical axis label)

Notice both the tremendous price fluctuation among stones of the same size due to differences in the flaw grades and color grades, and the disproportionate jumps in cost *per carat*, depending upon size.

84

Part Three

Colored Gemstones

11

The Mystery and Magic of Colored Gems

The world of colored gems is endlessly fascinating. Since ancient times, colored stones have been thought to possess certain magical powers or the ability to endow the wearer with certain attributes. Emeralds were thought to be good for the eyes; yellow stones were thought to cure jaundice; red stones to stop the flow of blood. At one time it was believed that a ruby worn by a man indicated command, nobility, lordship, and vengeance; worn by a woman, however, it indicated pride, obstinacy, and haughtiness. A blue sapphire worn by a man indicated wisdom, and high and magnanimous thoughts; on a woman, jealousy in love, politeness, and vigilance. The emerald signified for man joyousness, transitory hope, and the decline of friendship; for woman, unfounded ambition, childish delight, and change.

Colored gems, because of the magical powers associated with them, achieved extensive use as talismans and amulets; as predictors of the future; as therapeutic aids; and as essential elements to many religious practices—pagan, Hebrew, and Christian.

The following stones were strongly associated with the twelve tribes and the twelve apostles:

The Twelve Tribes of Israel

Levi—garnet	*Simeon*—chrysolite	*Reuben*—sard
Zebulon—diamond	(peridot)	(brown chalcedony)
Gad—amethyst	*Issachar*—sapphire	*Judah*—emerald
Benjamin—jasper	*Naphtali*—agate	*Dan*—topaz
	Joseph—onyx	*Asher*—beryl

The Twelve Apostles

Peter—jasper

Andrew—sapphire

James—chalcedony

John—emerald

Philip—sardonyx

Bartholomew—sard
   (brown chalcedony)

Matthew—chrysolite
   (peridot)

Thomas—beryl

James the Less—topaz

Jude—chrysoprase

Simon—hyacinth (zircon)

Judas—amethyst

The following is a list of the zodiacal gems passed on from very early history, and the powers or special characteristics attributed to each:

Aquarius (Jan. 21–Feb. 21)   **Garnet**—believed to guarantee true friendship when worn by an Aquarian

Pisces (Feb. 22–Mar. 21)   **Amethyst**—believed to protect a Pisces wearer from extremes of passion

Aries (Mar. 22–Apr. 20)   **Bloodstone**—believed to endow an Aries wearer with wisdom

Taurus (Apr. 21–May 21)   **Sapphire**—believed to protect from and cure mental disorders if worn by a Taurus

Gemini (May 22–June 21)   **Agate**—long life, health, and wealth were guaranteed to a Gemini if an agate ring was worn

Cancer (June 22–July 22)   **Emerald**—eternal joy was guaranteed to a Cancer-born if an emerald was taken with him on his way

Leo (July 23–Aug. 22)   **Onyx**—would protect a Leo wearer from loneliness and unhappiness

Virgo (Aug. 23–Sept. 22)   **Carnelian**—believed to guarantee success in anything a Virgo tried if worn on the hand of the Virgo

Libra (Sept. 23–Oct. 23)	**Chrysolite (peridot)**—would free a Libra wearer from any evil spell
Scorpio (Oct. 24–Nov. 21)	**Beryl**—should be worn by every Scorpio to guarantee protection from "tears of sad repentance"
Sagittarius (Nov. 22–Dec. 21)	**Topaz**—protects the Sagittarian, but only if the Sagittarian always shows a topaz
Capricorn (Dec. 22–Jan. 21)	**Ruby**—a Capricorn who has ever worn a ruby will never know trouble

The preceding list of zodiac signs is from a Hindu legend, but there are others. An old Spanish list, probably representing an Arab tradition, ascribes the following stones to the various signs of the zodiac:

Aquarius—Amethyst	*Leo*—Topaz
Pisces—(indistinguishable)	*Virgo*—Magnet (lodestone)
Aries—Crystal (quartz)	*Libra*—Jasper
Taurus—Ruby and diamond	*Scorpio*—Garnet
Gemini—Sapphire	*Sagittarius*—Emerald
Cancer—Agate and beryl	*Capricorn*—Chalcedony

It was believed that certain planets influenced stones, and that stones could therefore transmit the powers attributed to those planets. A further extension of this belief can be seen in the practice of engraving certain planetary constellations on stones. For example, a stone engraved with the two bears, Ursa Major and Ursa Minor, would make the wearer wise, versatile, and powerful. And so it went. And from such thought came the belief in birthstones.

The Evolution of Birthstones

The origin of the belief that a special stone was dedicated to each month and that the stone of the month possessed a special virtue or "cure" that it could transmit to those born in that month, goes back to at least the first century. There is speculation that the twelve stones in the great breastplate of the Jewish high priest may have had some bearing on this evolution. In the eighth and ninth centuries, the interpreters of Revelation began to ascribe to each of those stones attributes of the twelve apostles. The Hindus, on the other hand, had their interpretation.

But whatever the reason, one fact is clear. As G. F. Kunz points out, in *The Curious Lore of Precious Stones*, "there is no doubt that the owner of a ring or ornament set with a birthstone is impressed with the idea of possessing something more intimately associated with his or her personality than any other stone, however beautiful or costly. The idea that birthstones possess a certain indefinable, but none the less real significance has long been present, and still holds a spell over the minds of all who are gifted with a touch of imagination and romance."

Present-Day Birthstones

The following is the list of birthstones adopted in 1952 by major jewelry industry associations:

Month	Birthstone	Alternate Stone
January	Garnet	
February	Amethyst	
March	Bloodstone	Aquamarine
April	Diamond	
May	Emerald	
June	Pearl	Moonstone or Alexandrite
July	Ruby	
August	Sardonyx (carnelian)	Peridot
September	Sapphire	
October	Opal	Tourmaline
November	Topaz	Citrine
December	Turquoise	Zircon

Besides the lists of birthstones and zodiacal or talismanic stones, there are lists of stones for days of the week, hours of the day, for states of the union, for each of the seasons.

The Importance of Color and Its Mystical Symbolism in Gems

Yellow	Worn by a man, denoted secrecy (appropriate for a silent lover); worn by a woman, it indicated generosity.
White *(colorless)*	Signifies friendship, integrity, and religion for men; purity, affability, and contemplation for women.
Red	On a man, indicated command, nobility, lordship, and vengeance; on a woman, pride, haughtiness, and obstinacy.
Blue	On a man, indicated wisdom and high and magnanimous thoughts; on a woman, jealousy in love, politeness, vigilance.
Green	For men, signified joyousness, transitory hope, decline of friendship; for women, unfounded ambition, childish delight, and change.
Black	For men, meant gravity, good sense, constancy, and strength; for young women, fickleness and foolishness, but for married women, constant love and perseverance.
Violet	For men, sober judgment, industry, and gravity; for women, high thoughts and spiritual love.

What Colored Stones Are Available Today?

Today, gems are worn primarily for their intrinsic beauty and are chosen primarily for aesthetic reasons. While we may own a birthstone that we wear on occasion, our choice is dictated more by personal color preferences, economics, and fashion. The world of colored gems today offers us an almost endless choice. New gems have been discovered and are being made available through the major jewelry companies. If you like red, there are rubies, garnets, red tourmalines, red spinels, and even red diamonds. If you prefer blue, there are sapphires, iolite, blue spinel, blue topaz, blue tourmaline, tanzanite, and even blue diamonds. For those who prefer green, there are emeralds, tsavorite (green garnet), green zircons, green tourmalines, green sapphires, peridots, and even green diamonds.

The following chapters will discuss colored stones. We hope that the information will be helpful to you, not only increasing your knowledge about each stone, but also, and perhaps more importantly, making you aware of the *variety* of stones available today in every hue. There is a colored gem available to almost everyone, in almost any color, at almost any price. You have a wide range of affordable options. We hope the information provided here opens up many options for you in an ever more exciting world—the world of colored gems.

12

Determining Value in Colored Gems

Color is the principal determinant of value in colored gems. It is also, too often, the principal determinant in erroneous identification. Unfortunately, most people don't realize how many gems look alike in color. And often, dealers, too, can be misled or caught off-guard. Too often recognition and identification are based on color alone because so few, jewelers and customers alike, are aware of the large number of similarly colored stones that are available.

The trade has promoted very few colored stones until recently. Only now can consumers find they have a choice. If you want an emerald-green stone but can't afford a true emerald, you might choose a green garnet (tsavorite), a green sapphire, or a green tourmaline. As consumers become more knowledgeable about look-alikes, so will jewelers!

Color is affected by many variables that make it difficult to truly evaluate. Color is affected primarily by light—the type of light and its intensity. In addition, color can be very subjective in terms of what is considered pleasing and desirable. Nonetheless, there have been major studies in recent years to bring some degree of standardization to the colored-gem market. GIA now offers an instrument called the Color Master, which is a type of visual colorimeter (a color-grading machine). The American Gem Laboratory (AGL) has a color-scanning system to grade color. Both have their shortcomings at this time but are still of assistance in color grading. Nothing, however, can replace the eye-and-brain combination, coupled with years of experience in the colored-stone field.

As a general rule, the closer a stone comes to being the pure spectral hue of that color, the better the color. For example, if we are considering a green stone, the purer the green, the better the color. In other words, the closer it comes to being a pure spectral green, having no strong undertone of any other color such as blue or yellow, the better the color.

The Key Elements in Describing Color

The spectral colors go from pure red to pure violet, not including brown, white, black, and gray. It is these latter colors, in combination with the spectral colors, that affect the tone of the color seen and that make the classification of color so difficult. For example, if there is white present with red, you will have a lighter tone of red; if there is black, you will have a darker shade.

In describing color we will often refer to these factors:

- Hue—the precise spectral color
- Intensity—the brightness or vividness (or dullness or drabness) of the color
- Tone—the depth of color (light or dark)
- Distribution—the even (or uneven) distribution of the color

Both intensity and tone of color can be significantly affected by the proportioning of the cut. In other words, a good lapidary (gem cutter) working with a fine stone will be able to bring out its inherent, potential beauty to the fullest, making it very desirable. A poor cutter may take the same rough material and create a stone that is not really desirable, because a poor cut will significantly reduce the vividness and alter the depth of color, usually producing a stone that is much too dark to be attractive.

In general, stones that are either very light (pale) or very dark sell for less per carat. There seems to be a common belief that the darker the stone, the better. This is true only to a point. A rich, deep color is desirable, but not a depth of color that approaches black. The average consumer must shop around and train the eye to differentiate between a nice depth of color and a stone that is too dark.

As a general rule, it is even more important to shop around when considering colored stones than it is when buying diamonds. One must develop an eye for all of the variables of color—hue, intensity, tone, and distribution. Some stones simply exhibit a more intense, vivid color than other stones (all else being equal), but only by extensive visual comparison can you develop your own eye.

Let's discuss the ruby for a moment. The finest red rubies are Burmese. While they are not a pure red, these are the closest to pure red. The tone may vary, however, from very light to very dark. As with most stones, the very light stones and the very dark stones sell for less per carat. Burmese rubies are the most highly prized, and the most expensive, because of the desirability of their color and their scarcity.

Thai rubies can vary tremendously in hue and tone, going from a light to dark red with varying degrees of a blue undertone, giving them a purplish cast and making them look like the much cheaper reddish purple gemstone, the garnet. While some shades of Thai ruby are very expensive, most of these stones are much less expensive than the Burmese.

The African rubies, Tanzanian, have a tint or undertone of brown or orange, which makes them also much cheaper than the Burmese reds, but more valuable than the Thai ruby, depending on the color of the Thai ruby.

Ceylon rubies are also encountered with relative frequency. However, these are usually classified as pink sapphires and not as rubies, since the tone is consistently pale. The saturation of color is too weak to be technically described as ruby, since ruby must be deep red, not pink. In fact, it is a misnomer to call any pink ruby a ruby—if it's pink, it's a sapphire. (Sapphire and ruby are the same stone, physically and chemically. The red variety is called ruby, while the equally popular blue is called sapphire.)

Next, let's look at emeralds. Some of the finest emeralds today come from Colombia. The Colombian emerald is the color of fresh, young green grass—a pure spectral green with a faint tint of either yellow or blue. The "drop of oil" emerald from Colombia is considered absolutely the finest, and is a deep green (do not confuse with dark green, which has black in it) with a very slight blue undertone. This is the most valuable color and is unique to Colombian varieties.

The African emerald is also a nice shade of green, but it has a blue undertone with a slight darkening effect (probably due to traces of iron), which makes the stone less valuable than the Colombian. However, it usually has less flaws than the Colombian, and cuts a more vivid stone. Therefore, some of the African stones, depending on depth of color, compare very favorably to the Colombian, aesthetically, while costing less per carat.

Importance of Environment

The color of a stone can be drastically affected by the kind of light and the environment (color of wallpaper, color of shirt, etc.) in which the examination is being conducted. If examined under a fluorescent light, a ruby may not show its fullest red, because most fluorescent lights are weak in red rays, which will cause the red in the ruby to be diminished and to appear more *purple* red in body color. The same ruby examined in daylight or under incandescent light (ordinary electric light bulb), which is not weak in red rays, will appear a truer, fuller red. The same ruby would look even redder if examined against a piece of orange yellow paper. We wish to stress that the color of a ruby is definitely dependent upon the "color temperature" or type of light used, as well as the environment in which it is examined. Loose rubies are often shown in little envelopes, called "parcel papers," that have a yellow orange inner paper liner to enhance the red color to the fullest.

Blue sapphire is another intensely colored gem that needs discussion. Blue sapphire comes in numerous tones of blue—from light to very dark, some so dark that they look black in artificial light. Many contain some degree of green—the more green, the lower the price. Some even exhibit a color change, turning slightly lavender over time (such as the stones from the Umba Valley in Tanzania). The lighter blues are generally referred to as Ceylon sapphire; the finest and most expensive blue sapphires are Burmese, which exhibit a rich, true blue in all kinds of light; and some prefer the more subdued, soft, velvety-looking blue exhibited by the rare Kashmir sapphires, which are also very expensive.

A Word About Color Distribution or Zoning

Even though zoning doesn't really describe color, it is very important in evaluating color.

In some stones the color isn't always evenly distributed but may exist in zones—adding color to colorless areas surrounding the zone. This is frequently observed in amethyst, ruby, and sapphire. These zones may be observed by looking through the side of the stone, moving it slowly, while tilting it and rotating it.

Sometimes a stone in the rough is colorless, or nearly so, but has a spot or layer of color. If the cutter cuts the stone so that the culet is in the color spot, the whole stone will appear that color. If there is a layer and the cutter cuts the stone so that the layer lies in a plane nearly parallel to the table, the whole stone will look completely colored. Evenness of color and complete saturation of color are very important in determining the value of colored gems.

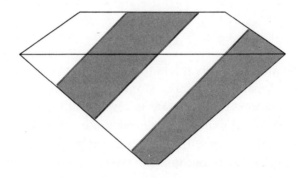

Zones of color in a stone

Another example showing how strongly the color seen can be affected by the type of light in which it is observed is found with the gem alexandrite (even with the inexpensive synthetic corundum, often sold erroneously as alexandrite.) Alexandrite can be a bluish green gem in daylight or under daylight-type fluorescent light, and a deep red or purple red under incandescent light (an ordinary electric light bulb).

An emerald-cut emerald mounted in a normal four-prong setting will not appear to have as deep a color as the same emerald if mounted in a special type of setting or box that makes a complete, deep enclosure preventing light from entering the sides of the stone. The "shadowy" effect of this enclosure deepens the color of the stone. This technique, and other types of special mounting, can be used to improve the color of any colored gemstone where it is desirable to deepen or intensify the color. Another example is found with fine expensive imperial jade. Fine jade cabochons (a rounded, oval stone without facets) are often mounted with a solid rim around the girdle (bezel set), with the back of the ring being constructed much deeper than the actual bottom of the stone, and the back side of the ring nearly completely closed except for a small opening at the bottom center. Since gold is expensive, this is done either to hide a stone's defect or to improve its body color.

Opal will provide another example. The environment in this case is a blackened, closed, flat back, which intensifies the play of color (fire) seen in opal.

Clarity

As with diamonds, *clarity* refers to the absence of internal flaws (inclusions). Flawlessness in colored stones is perhaps even rarer than in diamonds. However, while clarity is important, and the cleaner the stone the better, flawlessness in colored stones does not usually carry the premium that it does with diamonds. Light, pastel-colored stones will require better clarity because the flaws are more readily visible in these stones; in darker-toned stones the flaws may not be as important a variable because they are masked by the depth of color.

The type and placement of flaws is a more important consideration in colored stones than the presence of flaws in and of themselves. For example, a large crack (called a *feather*) that is close to the surface of a stone can be dangerous because it weakens the stone's durability and breaks the light continuity. Also, it may show an iridescent effect that could detract from its beauty. (Iridescence usually means that a fracture or feather breaks through the surface somewhere on the stone.) Such a flaw would certainly reduce the stone's value. But if the fracture is small and positioned in an unobtrusive part of the stone, it will have minimal effect on its durability, beauty, and value. Some flaws actually help a gemologist or jeweler to identify a stone. There are also certain types of flaws that are characteristic of specific gems and specific localities and, again, may detract only minimally from the value. In some cases the presence of a particular flaw may provide positive identification of the exact variety or origin and actually cause an *increase* in the per-carat value. We should note, however, that a very fine colored gem that really is flawless will probably bring a disproportionately *much higher* price per carat because it is so rare.

Types of Flaws Found in Colored Gems

There are numerous types of flaws found in colored gems. Since certain types are found in some gems but not in others, they provide the gemologist with an important means of positive identification in many cases. Types of flaws a gemologist will look for include the following:

Needle- or fiber-like inclusions. Some of these types of inclusions can be found in garnet, sapphire, ruby, aquamarine, and amethyst.

Two-phase inclusions. This is an inclusion that has a "frankfurter" outline with an enclosed bubble—which may or may not move as the "frank" is tilted from end to end. These can be observed in topaz, quartz, synthetic emeralds, and sometimes tourmalines.

Three-phase inclusions. These look like irregularly shaped pea pods, usually pointed at both ends, containing a bubble and a cube shape or rhomboid solid adjacent to the bubble. The three-phase inclusion may be liquid (pea pod), solid (cube or rhomboid), or gas (bubble). These are found in genuine Colombian emeralds, verifying the emeralds' origin and genuineness.

Twinning planes. These are found in rubies and sapphires and occasionally in some of the feldspar gems (such as moonstone). They have the appearance of parallel cracks that resemble panes of glass lying in parallel planes. In rubies and sapphires these can often be found to crisscross at 60° and 120° to each other. These types of inclusions can prove the genuineness of a ruby or sapphire, but if too numerous they may both weaken the stone and diminish its brilliance.

Liquid-filled or healing feather. This type of inclusion is found in the corundum family, although it is more frequently observed in sapphires than in rubies. It is frequently shaped like a maze.

Veils. Small bubblelike inclusions arranged in a layerlike formation that can be flat or curvaceous, broad or narrow, long or short. These may be easily observed in some synthetic emeralds.

Fingerprint. These are small crystal inclusions that are arranged in curved rows in such a way as to resemble a fingerprint or maze design. They can be seen in quartz and topaz. They closely resemble the liquid-filled healing feathers seen in rubies and sapphires.

Dark ball-like inclusions. These are found exclusively in Thai rubies. They are dark, opaque balls surrounded by an irregularly shaped, wispy, brown cloudlike formation. These are never seen in Burmese stones (which often contain needlelike inclusions never seen in Thai stones).

Cleavage fault. This is a type of break in the stone rather than an actual inclusion. It is observed in topaz, diamond, feldspar, kunzite, hiddenite. It is a plane-type crack and can weaken the stone if it is exposed to extreme temperature change (thermoshock) or struck a severe blow, which could break the stone apart.

Bubbles. Nice round bubbles usually indicate a synthetic or glass, though they can be found in amber. In synthetic corundum (ruby, sapphire) they can be round, pear-shaped, or tadpole-shaped. In the latter two, the points of the pear and the tail of the tadpole always point in the same direction.

Curved striae. These are concentric curved lines seen in synthetic sapphire and synthetic ruby, made by older processes, but are difficult to observe in light-colored stones, such as pale synthetic pink or yellow sapphire.

Swirl marks. These are found in glass. They appear in serpentine or curved shapes and curlicues, and usually appear as a darker shade of color.

Halo or disklike inclusions. Many of the Ceylon sapphires contain flat, disklike inclusions, sometimes referred to as halos. Very often they will contain a small black mark at the center, and sometimes a crystal can be seen, rather than a black mark. These are small zircon crystals that cause the formation of these halos.

If the flaws weaken the stone's durability, affect color, are easily noticeable, or are too numerous, they will significantly reduce price. Otherwise, they may not affect price to any great extent at all. And in some cases, if they provide positive identification and proof of origin, they may actually have a positive effect on price, increasing the cost rather than reducing it (as with Burmese rubies and Colombian emeralds). It is also true that flawless colored stones are rare, and so may bring a disproportionately much higher price per carat.

Again, as a consumer it is important to shop around and become familiar with the stone you wish to purchase and to train your eye to discern what is acceptable or objectionable.

The Importance of Cut

As stated earlier, cut and proportion in colored stones is important for two main reasons:

1. It affects the *depth* of color seen in the stone.
2. It affects the *liveliness* projected by the stone.

Color and cut are the most important criteria in determining value in colored stones, after which carat weight must be factored in—the higher carat weight will usually increase the price per carat, and usually in a nonlinear proportionality. If a colored stone was of good-quality material to begin with, a good cut will enhance its natural beauty to the fullest and allow it to exhibit its finest color and liveliness. If we take the same material and cut it poorly, its natural beauty will be lessened, causing it to look too dark, or too light, or even "dead."

Therefore, when we examine a colored stone that looks lively to our eye and has good color—not too dark and not too pale—we can assume the cut is reasonably good. If the stone's color is poor, or if it lacks liveliness, we must immediately examine it for proper cut. If it has been cut properly, we can assume the basic material was poor. However, if the cut is poor, the material may be very good and can perhaps be recut into a beautiful gem. In this case we may want to confer with a knowledgeable cutter to see if it is worthwhile to recut, considering cutting costs and loss in weight. If you don't know any cutters, a reputable jeweler, gemologist-appraiser, or local lapidary club may be able to recommend one.

What to Consider If the Cut and Proportion of a Colored Stone Look Good

Is the shade pleasing, and does the stone have life and brilliance? If the answer is yes to both considerations, then the basic material is probably good, and you must make a decision based on your own personal preferences and budget.

Is the color too light or too dark? If so, and if the cut looks good, the basic uncut material was probably too light or too dark. Avoid purchasing such stones for investment. Consider purchase if personally pleasing, but only if the price is right (significantly lower than stones of better color).

Is its brilliance even, or are there dead spots or flat areas? If the brilliance is not uniform, or the stone looks dead or flat, avoid purchasing. The cut may look good, but probably is not right for the particular stone. For example, tourmaline in a normal emerald cut may look flat, while special faceting on the back facets can add tremendous brilliance. But the average consumer can't really determine to what extent the cut is responsible for the flatness and to what extent it's due to poor quality, rough material.

What to Consider If Cut and Proportion in a Colored Stone Are Thick

Is the color dark? This is usually the case. In a thick stone, however, it is possible that the original material was of good color tone and that the cut has created the undesirable darkness. The cost of this stone should be less per carat than one less dark, and it may, therefore, be feasible to purchase it (if the price is sufficiently low) and invest in re-cutting the stone to a more ideal proportion to enhance its natural color. While the size would be reduced, the price per carat would be increased. At worst, there would be a trade-off—reduced size for increased beauty and increased price per carat. In some cases the price per carat may increase so substantially that the overall value of the stone, even though smaller, also increases substantially.

This is often true with African and Oriental stones. African and Oriental cutters have a tendency to cut for maximum carat weight, resulting in stones that are too deep and therefore look thick, heavy, very dark, and often lifeless. While many of these stones are undesirable in these "native cuts," they can be recut into lively stones with a much more pleasing color, which then take on much greater beauty and desirability. And again, even though the recutting reduces the size, the price per carat increases, resulting in a stone that may actually be more valuable than the larger stone before recutting.

What to Consider If Cut and Proportion in a Colored Stone Are Shallow

Is the stone's color too light? This is often the case. Light stones sell for less per carat. If the color is pleasing to your personal taste, and priced fairly, it may be a good purchase. It may, however, be more difficult to resell at some future time. It is usually not economically feasible to try to recut shallow stones to enhance their color.

Is it lively? Usually, while a shallowly cut stone can exhibit a nice color, it will lack liveliness.

Is the stone cut so shallow that its wearability is reduced? If the stone is cut too shallow, it may be unwearable. For example, it may not be feasible to wear it in a ring, although it may be worn with reasonable safety in a pendant, or as earrings, since these types of jewelry are less exposed to blows or knocks and their subsequent damage.

Will this stone be worn frequently and be prone to collecting dirt or grease? In shallowly cut pastel or light-colored stones, such as aquamarine, zircon, amethyst, and topaz, the apparent body color and brilliance are diminished considerably if grease or dirt collects on the back side. This is often the case with a ring worn daily and subjected to cooking, dishwashing, cosmetic application, bath oils, etc. These stones should be frequently and properly cleaned, or should not be purchased.

Weight

As with diamonds, weight is measured in carats. Before 1913 the carat weight varied depending upon the country of origin—the Indian carat didn't weigh the same as the English carat; the French carat was different from the Indian or English. This is important if you have or are thinking of buying a very old piece that still has the original bill of sale indicating carat weight—the old carat weighed more than the new (since 1913) metric carat, which is 200 milligrams (⅕ gram). Therefore, an old "3-carat" stone will weigh more than 3 carats by the new standards. The use of *metric* is often deleted today, and we simply refer to the carat, meaning the 200-milligram carat.

All gems are weighed in carats, except pearls and coral. (Pearls and coral are sold by the grain, momme, and millimeter. A grain is ¼ carat; a momme is 18.75 carats.)

Normally, the greater the weight, the greater the value per carat, unless we reach unusually large sizes—in excess of 50 carats, after which size may become prohibitive for use in some types of jewelry (rings or earrings), and price per carat may drop because liquidity is more difficult (unless it is a rare stone in that size). There are genuine cut topazes weighing from 2,500 to 12,000 carats, which could be used as paperweights.

Also, remember again not to confuse *weight* with *size*. Some stones weigh more than others; the density (specific gravity) of the basic material is heavier. A 1-carat ruby will have a different size than a 1-carat emerald or a 1-carat diamond.

Some stones are readily available in large sizes (over 10 carats), such as tourmaline. For other stones, sizes over 5 carats may be very rare and therefore considered large, and will also command a proportionately higher price (precious topaz, alexandrite, demantoid and tsavorite garnets, ruby, and red beryl). With these stones a 10-carat stone can command any price—a king's ransom. A 30-carat blue diamond was sold in 1982 for $9 million.

Scarcity of certain sizes among the different colored stones affects the definition of "large" in the colored-gem market. A fine 5-carat alexandrite or ruby is a very large stone; an 18-carat tourmaline is a nice sized stone.

As with diamonds, stones under 1 carat sell for less per carat than stones of 1 carat or more. But here it becomes more complicated. The definition of "large" or "rare" sizes differs tremendously, as does price depending upon the stone. For example, an 8-carat tourmaline is an average-size stone, fairly common, and will be priced accordingly. A 5-carat tsavorite is extremely rare, and will command a price proportionately much greater than a 1-carat stone. Precious topaz used to be readily available in 20-carat sizes and larger, but today even 10-carat stones of very fine color are practically nonexistent and their price has jumped tremendously.

A colored-gemstone chart in Chapter 14 indicates the availability of stones in large sizes, indicating where scarcity may exist and at what size.

13

Fraud and Misrepresentation in Colored Gems

Before we begin this chapter, we would like to reemphasize here, as we did in the chapter on diamonds, that as a percentage of total jewelry transactions, the occurrence of misrepresentation and fraud is low, and that most jewelers are reputable professionals in whom you can place your trust.

However, in the colored gem market there is a greater occurrence of misrepresentation than in the diamond market, primarily because of the scientifically complex nature of colored stones. So it is even more important for you to be aware of the deceptive practices one might encounter when buying a colored gem, both to protect yourself from the more obvious scams, and to better understand the importance of dealing with a reliable jeweler. We stress the importance, also, to an even greater degree, of seeking verification from a qualified gemologist—one with extensive experience with colored gems we might add—when buying any expensive colored gem.

Take precaution that your gemstone is what it is represented to be.

Misrepresenting Synthetic as Natural

Today there is much misrepresentation of the synthetic as natural. Synthetic gems have been manufactured for many years. Good synthetic sapphires, rubies, and spinels have been manufactured since the early 1900s. Very good synthetic emeralds began to be produced commercially in the 1940s. These synthetics, while they looked like the real thing to the average consumer and were very attractive because of their affordable price, could be *readily* distinguished from the real thing by a competent jeweler.

Today, this may not be the case, particularly with ruby and emerald. While the older techniques for producing these synthetics are still used, new sophisticated methods have enabled the production of synthetic rubies and emeralds that are *not* readily discernible, because they do not possess the familiar characteristics common to the older type synthetics, with which the dealer and jeweler are so familiar. This is particularly true with the new synthetic ruby, which is especially difficult to differentiate from its natural counterpart. Many have been represented and sold as genuine. A highly qualified gemologist can, however, differentiate between these new, fine synthetics and natural stones. Let me tell you a story that dramatically illustrates today's situation.

We know a jeweler with an excellent reputation for being honest, reliable, and expert in his field. He had been in the business for many years and had extensive gemological training. Nonetheless, he recently sold a new-synthetic ruby as a natural ruby for just under $10,000.

His customer, who had purchased the stone at a reasonable price, proceeded to resell it to a third party for a quick profit. The third party took it to a very competent gemologist whom he knew to be up-to-date on the scientific procedures necessary to differentiate even the new synthetics from natural rubies. And the truth was learned!

The second and third parties in this case lost nothing (one of the benefits of buying from a reputable jeweler). However, the jeweler suffered both a heavy financial loss and heavy damage to his reputation.

You may ask how he made such a mistake. It was easy. He was knowledgeable, like many other jewelers, and thought he knew how to distinguish a natural from a synthetic. But he had not kept current on the new technological advances and the new synthetics entering the marketplace. So he made the purchase of this lovely stone over-the-counter from a private party who had procured it in the Orient. These new synthetic rubies are produced in the United States and then "find their way" to the Orient—the source of the naturals—where they are more easily sold as the real thing. And he had no recourse at all, because he had no way of locating the seller, who had simply walked in off the street.

As this story illustrates, today it is essential for the consumer to have a highly qualified gemologist verify authenticity—particularly with fine rubies. Thousands of dollars may be at stake, for too many jewelers innocently represent these new synthetics as genuine because they themselves bought them as genuine. Don't delude yourself into believing that if a piece is purchased from a well-respected firm it must therefore be what it is represented to be. It may be inconvenient, and it may require an additional charge, but we believe it is better to be safe now than sorry later.

With today's sophisticated equipment, and a greater knowledge of crystals, it is possible for man to create almost any gemstone. For example, synthetic alexandrite has been successfully produced since 1973, and is another example of a gem that is difficult to distinguish from its natural counterpart. These gemstones, though not as expensive as the genuine, are also not inexpensive themselves.

As a general rule, remember that almost any expensive gem—opals, alexandrite, ruby, emerald, sapphire, and even turquoise—today *could* be a synthetic, that many synthetics are themselves expensive, and that most have become more difficult to distinguish from their natural counterparts, so there is innocent "confusion" and subsequent "misrepresentation" by the jeweler. *Make sure you take proper precaution* to guarantee that the gem you're considering is as represented.

Simulated Stones

These should not be confused with synthetics. A simulated stone is usually a very inexpensive man-made stone. It is usually glass, but can also be plastic. These stones simulate the stone's color only and are very easily differentiated from the genuine. There are glass simulations of all the colored stones, and glass and plastic simulated pearls, turquoise, and amber are among the most common.

Color Alteration—Heating, Radiation, Dyeing, and Other Techniques

Heat Treatment

Heat treatment is the most commonly encountered method of changing a gem's color. Subjecting certain stones to sophisticated heating procedures changes or enhances their color. The treatment may lighten, darken, or completely change the color. This procedure is commonly applied to the following stones:

Zircon—to produce blue or colorless stones

Amethyst—to produce "yellow" stones sold as citrine and topaz; "green" sold as praseolite

Topaz—to produce shades of blue or pink

Sapphire—to lighten the blue color; to darken a light color; or to change the lavender shades to pink

Aquamarine—to deepen the blue color

Tanzanite—to produce a more desirable shade of blue

Tourmaline—to lighten the darker shades (usually of the green variety)

Morganite—to change the color from orange to pinkish lavender

The color obtained by these heating procedures is usually permanent.

Radiation

Radiation techniques are now in common use, produced by any of several methods, each of which has a specific application. Sometimes radiation is used in combination with heat treatment. Radiation techniques are used for the following stones:

Aquamarine—to deepen its color (often in conjunction with heat)

Diamond—to change the color from an off-white color to a fancy color—green, yellow, etc.

Sapphire—to produce the beautiful golden-colored sapphire seen today

Topaz—to change from colorless or nearly colorless to blue

Some of the blue topazes have been found to be radioactive and may be harmful to the wearer. A Geiger counter should be used to determine whether a stone possesses harmful levels of radioactivity.

As far as we know now, the color changes resulting from radiation treatment are usually permanent. We know of one exception. Nice "yellow" sapphires that have obtained their color by radiation treatment will lose their color if heated by the flame of a common cigarette lighter. If you are considering a "yellow," it may be worthwhile to try this simple flame test if the jeweler will permit (he probably won't, however).

The color of fancy colored diamonds can usually be verified as being natural or radiated. However, with most other radiated stones identification procedures for determining whether color is natural have not been developed as of this date.

Dyeing

Dyeing has been practiced since earliest times, particularly with the less expensive gemstone called chalcedony (a variety of quartz). The gems frequently dyed are jade, opal, coral, lapis, and to a lesser degree poor-quality star rubies, star sapphires, and emeralds.

Chalcedony—dyed to produce "black onyx," which does not occur naturally; banded agate variety showing white bands alternating with strong colored bands; dyed reddish brown to sell as carnelian (which also occurs naturally); dyed green to represent chrysoprase (which also occurs naturally)

Jade (jadeite)—color frequently improved by dyeing to a beautiful emerald or young grass green color, to look like "imperial" jade. While jade occurs naturally in almost every color, it may also be dyed to other colors.

Coral and lapis—dyed to deepen the color, or create more uniform color

Swiss lapis—jasper is often dyed blue and sold as "lapis" or "Swiss lapis"

Other Coloring Techniques

Blackening techniques. These are used to alter color, not by dyeing but by introducing a chemical reaction (sugar-acid chemical reaction) that introduces black carbon, which blackens the color. The following stones are commonly exposed to this treatment:

Opal—to blacken so as to resemble the more valuable, precious black opal

Black onyx—chalcedony is blackened by this technique to create black onyx, which does not occur in nature

Waxing. This is a process consisting of rubbing the stone with a tinted waxlike substance to hide surface cracks and blemishes and to slightly improve the color. This is used primarily for the cheaper Indian star rubies, or sometimes on star sapphires.

Oiling. This technique is commonly used on emeralds. The emerald is soaked in oil (which may or may not be tinted green). Its purpose is to fill fine cracks, which are fairly common in emerald. These cracks look whitish and therefore weaken the green body color of the emerald. The oil fills the cracks, making them "disappear," and thereby improves the color by eliminating the white.

This is an accepted procedure and will normally last for many years. However, if the stone is put in a hot ultrasonic cleaner (which is dangerous to any emerald and *never* recommended), or soaked in an organic solvent such as gasoline, xylene, or substances containing these, such as paint remover, the oil may be slowly dissolved out of the cracks and the whitish blemishes will then reappear and the stone's color will be weakened. If this should happen, the stone can be reoiled.

Painting. This technique is often used with cabochon-cut transparent ("jelly") or semitransparent opals to create a stone that looks like the precious black opal. This is done by putting the stone set in a closed-back setting that has a high rim (bezel). A black cement or paint is placed on the inside of the setting so that when the opal is placed inside, the light is trapped, reflects from the back, and gives the opal the appearance of a fine black opal. (See also section, below, describing composite stones and opal doublets.)

Foil-backed stones. This technique is not frequently encountered, but should be mentioned. It is used primarily in cabochon-cut stones, but can be used on any stone, set usually in a closed-back mounting. This technique involves lining the inside of the setting with a colored foil that projects the color into the stone, deepening its color. *Always be apprehensive when considering a piece of jewelry that has a closed back.* This technique has been observed in both antique and modern jewelry.

We recently examined a heavy, yellow-gold cross set with five fine, flawless emeralds of a gem-green body color. The stones were set into the gold and therefore the backs were not observable. Suspicion arose since the emeralds were all flawless and the color was so uniformly fine. Upon examination it was discovered that the green body color was projected into the stones by a fine emerald-green foil back. The stones were probably not even emerald, but almost colorless aquamarines. Since both aquamarine and emerald belong to the same mineral family (beryl), an inexperienced jeweler or gemologist using normal, basic procedures to identify the stones could have erroneously identified them as fine emeralds.

Smoking. This is a technique used only on opals. It is used to turn off-white to tan colored opals from Mexico into a more desirable, moderately dark coffee brown body color that greatly enhances the opal fire.

It consists of taking the cut and polished opal, wrapping it tightly in brown paper, and putting it in a covered container over moderate heat until the paper is completely charred. When cooled and removed, the opal now has a much more intense brown body color and fire. But if this smoke-produced color coating were to be badly scratched, the underlying color would show through and the stone would have to be resmoked.

This can be easily detected by wetting the stone (preferably with saliva). While wet, some of the fire disappears, and then reappears after the surface has dried.

Composite Stones

Composite stones are exactly what the term implies—a stone composed of more than one part. There are two types of composite stones we will mention—doublets and triplets.

Doublets are composite stones consisting of two parts, sometimes held together by a colored cement.

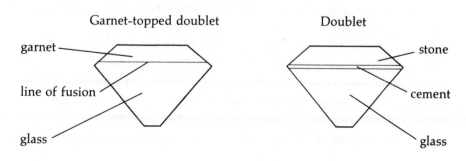

Garnet-topped doublet   Doublet

garnet —   line of fusion   glass   stone — cement — glass

Triplets are composite stones consisting of three parts, usually glued together to a colored middle part.

Triplet

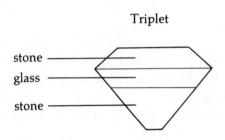

stone ——
glass ——
stone ——

Doublets

Doublets are especially important to know about, since they were so widely used in antique jewelry before the production of synthetics.

The most commonly encountered doublet, often referred to as a *false doublet*, consisted of a red garnet top fused to an appropriately colored glass bottom. With the right combination, any gem could be simulated by this method. For example, blue sapphire was created by fashioning a doublet that consisted of a red garnet top and a blue glass bottom. An emerald could be created by fusing the red garnet top to a green glass bottom. And so it went.

Garnets were used for the top halves of these false doublets because they possessed nice luster and excellent durability and were readily available in great quantity, which made them very inexpensive.

There are also doublets made from two parts of a gem, usually a colorless stone cemented together in the middle with an appropriately colored glue. For example, a colorless synthetic spinel top and bottom, held together in the middle (at the girdle) by red, green, or blue glue to simulate ruby, emerald, or sapphire.

There are also blue sapphire doublets (called *true doublets*) in circulation that are composed of two parts of genuine sapphire—but a genuine pale *yellow* sapphire. The top and bottom are pale yellow sapphire cemented with blue glue, resulting in a very fine "blue sapphire." These are especially convincing as the "real thing."

Another type of sapphire doublet is composed of a genuine pale

Fancy diamonds of various colors, tones, and hues.

A fine, round, brilliant-cut diamond.

Diamonds showing popular fancy cuts, including marquis, emerald, oval, and pear shapes.

Yellow-colored gemstones. Pendant: rutile. *Clockwise from top:* yellow zircon, precious topaz, yellow sapphire, yellow zircon, golden beryl, yellow diamond, yellow garnet, citrine quartz (citrine "topaz"). Comparative price ranges for one-carat stones of comparable quality: topaz, $90-$500; sapphire, $100-$400; zircon, $60-$100; beryl, $50-$200; diamond (treated), $1,500-$5,000; diamond (natural), $5,000-$45,000; garnet, $100-$200; citrine, $6-$25.

Red-colored gemstones. *Top row, left to right:* garnet, ruby ring, spinel. *Middle row, left to right:* ruby, spinel, spinel. *Bottom:* rubellite tourmaline. Comparative price ranges for one-carat stones of comparable quality: garnet, $10–$50; ruby, $800–$45,000; spinel, $2,400–$3,000; rubellite tourmaline, $100–$400.

Green-colored gemstones. *Top row, left to right:* tourmaline, emerald and diamond ring, tourmaline. *Middle row, left to right:* peridot, emerald, tsavorite garnet. *Bottom:* emerald. Comparative price ranges for one-carat stones of comparable quality: tourmaline, $40–$600; tsavorite garnet, $1,000–$3,500; emerald, $500–$10,000; peridot, $30–$200.

Blue-colored gemstones. *Center:* Burmese sapphire ring. *Clockwise from top:* blue spinel, Australian sapphire, iolite ("water sapphire"), tanzanite, Ceylon sapphire, indicolite tourmaline, Ceylon sapphire, Australian sapphire. Comparative price ranges for one-carat stones of comparable quality: Burmese sapphire, $1,600–$8,500; blue spinel, $50–$200; iolite, $40–$85; Ceylon sapphire, $900–$6,000; tanzanite, $400–$1,000; indicolite tourmaline, $100–$500; Australian sapphire, $300–$1,800.

Tourmaline bracelet with seed pearls. Each tourmaline is a different color, showing shades of pink, green, gold, or blue. Tourmaline comes in almost every color.

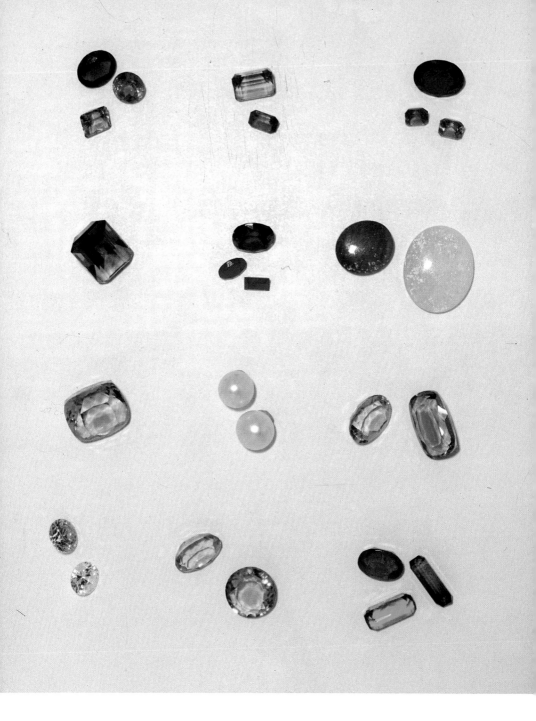

Popular birthstones. *Top to bottom, row 1:* garnet (January), amethyst (February), aquamarine (March), diamond (April); *row 2:* emerald (May), ruby (July), pearl (June), peridot (August); *row 3:* sapphire (September), opal (October), topaz (November), tourmaline (December).

yellow sapphire top fused to a *synthetic blue sapphire bottom. This would fool many a gemologist because four tests would provide positive ID as a genuine sapphire.*

The same techniques are used to make ruby doublets, although the ruby doublets don't look as convincing. And the same basic techniques can also be used to make emerald doublets (using beryl instead of sapphire). There are also opal doublets. These usually consist of a thin top layer of genuine opal cemented to a base that can be either a poorer grade of opal or some other substance altogether.

The most commonly encountered opal doublets are those made to look like the precious black opal. This doublet is usually composed of a translucent or transparent top that is cemented by black cement to a bottom portion of cheaper opal or other material that acts as a support. Please note that the top of these "black opal" doublets is usually never genuine black opal, though they certainly look like it.

Opal doublets are also made by cementing a thin piece of fine opal to a larger piece of less fine opal to create a larger overall appearance. The doublets can be identified by observing the join of the two pieces at the girdle and noting the dark line of the cement between the two pieces.

Triplets

Triplets are frequently encountered in the opal market and have substantially replaced the doublet. It is exactly like the opal doublet except that it has a cabochon-shaped colorless quartz cap (the third part) that covers the entire doublet, giving the delicate doublet greater protection from breakage and providing greater luminescence (brightness) to the stone.

With careful examination a competent jeweler or gemologist should be able to easily differentiate a doublet or triplet from a natural. We should note, however, that detection of an opal doublet may be very difficult if it is set in a mounting with a rim (bezel set) covering the seam where the two pieces are cemented together. It might be necessary to remove the stone from its setting for positive identification. (Removal must be performed only by a very competent manufacturing jeweler, due to opal's fragile nature—and he may do it only at your own risk, not wanting to assume responsibility for any breakage.) In the case of a black opal worth several thousand dollars, it is well worth the additional cost and inconvenience to be sure it is not a doublet worth only a few hundred dollars. *Always* be apprehensive of a flat-topped opal that is bezel-set.

Misleading Names

Many colored stones are called by names that lead one to believe they are something they are not. This practice is frequently encountered, especially outside the United States. When any stone is described with a qualifier, as in "Rio Topaz" or "Ceylon Sapphire," be sure to ask whether the stone is genuine, natural stone, and whether or not the color is natural. Ask why there is a qualifier.

Let's examine these two examples. In the case of Rio topaz, the stone is not a topaz at all, but a heat-treated amethyst, and the name, therefore, is clearly misleading. However, in the case of the Ceylon sapphire, "Ceylon" refers to the location from which that gem was mined, and Ceylons are always a particular tone of blue (a lighter shade, and very lively). Furthermore, because of their particular color, Ceylon sapphires sell for more per carat than certain other varieties, such as Australian or Thai. Therefore, in this case, "Ceylon" is very important to the stone's complete description.

Let's look at one more example, the Ceylon-colored sapphire. In this case, the qualifier is the word "colored." In most cases the presence of this word implies some type of color alteration or treatment. A Ceylon-colored sapphire is not a Ceylon sapphire but a sapphire that has been treated to obtain the Ceylon color.

There is nothing actually wrong with selling "Rio topaz" or "Ceylon-colored sapphire," or other similarly named stones, *as long as they are properly represented and priced.* Then the decision becomes yours— either you like it or you don't; it meets your emotional need for a topaz or Ceylon sapphire or it doesn't; and the price is right or it isn't. The following lists provide some examples of names to be aware of— "descriptive" names that are important to the stone's complete description; and "misleading" names, misnomers, which are meant to do exactly that, mislead:

Descriptive Names	Misnomers (and What They Really Are)

DIAMOND

Descriptive Names	Misnomers (and What They Really Are)
Canary diamond (refers to fancy yellow color) *Fancy Diamond* (refers to colored diamond)	*Alaska black diamond* (hematite) *Alaska diamond* (hematite) *Arkansas diamond* (quartz) *Black diamond* (hematite) *Bohemian diamond* (quartz) *Brazilian diamond* (quartz) (Diamond is also found in Brazil but is not referred to as "Brazilian diamond," but simply as "diamond.") *Bristol diamond* (quartz) *Buxton diamond* (quartz) *Cape May diamond* (quartz) *Ceylon diamond* (zircon) *Hawaiian diamond* (quartz) *Herkimer diamond* (quartz) *Kenya diamond* (rutile) *Matura diamond* (zircon) *Mogok diamond* (topaz) *Pennsylvania diamond* (pyrite) *Radium diamond* (smoky quartz) *Rainbow diamond* (rutile) *Rangoon diamond* (zircon) *Rhine diamond* (quartz; original rhinestone)

EMERALD

Descriptive Names	Misnomers (and What They Really Are)
Colombian emerald (refers to the finest variety of emerald, mined in Colombia)	*African emerald* (green fluorite) *Brazilian emerald* (tourmaline) (Genuine emerald is also found in Brazil; slightly different from Colombian emeralds, but called emerald rather than Brazilian emerald) *Chatham emerald* (synthetic) *Esmeralda emerald* (green tourmaline)

Descriptive Names	Misnomers (and What They Really Are)
(Emerald cont.)	*Evening emerald* (peridot)
	Gilson emerald (synthetic)
	Lechleitner emerald (partially synthetic)
	Lithia emerald (green spodumene—hiddenite)
	Mascot emerald (doublet)
	Oriental emerald (green sapphire)
	Soude emerald (doublet)
	Zerfass emerald (synthetic)

JADE

Descriptive Names	Misnomers (and What They Really Are)
Ax stone (nephrite jade)	*African jade* (green massive garnet)
California jade (both jadeite and nephrite jade)	*Amazon jade* (microcline feldspar; amazonite)
Greenstone (nephrite jade, New Zealand)	*Australian jade* (chrysoprase quartz)
Imperial jade (fine, gem-quality jadeite jade)	*California jade* (a variety of idocrase)
Jade (both nephrite jade and jadeite jade)	*Colorado jade* (amazonite feldspar)
Kidney stone (nephrite jade)	*Fukien jade* (soapstone)
Maori (nephrite jade from New Zealand)	*Honan jade* (soapstone)
Spinach jade (nephrite jade)	*Indian jade* (aventurine quartz)
	Jadine jade (Australian chrysoprase)
	Korea jade (serpentine [bowenite])
	Manchurian jade (soapstone)
	Mexican jade (dyed green calcite)
	New jade (serpentine [bowenite])
	Oregon jade (dark green jasper [quartz])
	Pennsylvania jade (serpentine, variety williamsite)
	Potomac jade (massive green diopside, Md., U.S.A.)

116

Descriptive Names	Misnomers (and What They Really Are)
	Soochow jade (serpentine or soap-stone)
	Styrian jade (pseudophite)
	Swiss jade (dyed green jasper [quartz])
	Virginia jade (amazonite, variety of feldspar)

PEARLS

Descriptive Names	Misnomers (and What They Really Are)
Oriental pearl (genuine, natural pearl)	*Atlas pearls* (imitation—satinspar type gypsum beads)
Cultured pearl (pearl made by man's implanting a bead into the oyster, which then covers the bead with the pearl substance, nacre. Can't be differentiated from natural pearl except by X ray or very strong microscopic examination).	*Laguna pearls* (imitation)
	La Jausca pearls (imitation)
	Nassau pearls (pink conch pearl, common and usually inexpensive)
	Patona pearls (pink conch pearl)
Biwa pearl (a cultured pearl, lacking the "bead" implantation, grown in lakes rather than salt water. These can be produced more easily and more quickly than the saltwater pearl).	*Patricia pearls* (pink conch pearl)
	Pompadour pearls (pink conch pearl)
	Red Sea pearls (coral beads)
	Tecla pearls (pink conch pearl)

RUBY

Descriptive Names	Misnomers (and What They Really Are)
African ruby (ruby from Africa)	*Adelaide ruby* (garnet, Australia)
Burma ruby (ruby from Burma—most desirable red color; most expensive)	*Albandine ruby* (garnet)
	Ancona ruby (quartz)
	Australian ruby (garnet)
Ceylon ruby (ruby from Sri Lanka [Ceylon])	*Balas ruby* (spinel)
	Bohemian ruby (garnet)
Thai ruby (ruby from Thailand)	*Brazilian ruby* (tourmaline)
	Brazilian ruby (topaz; rare)
	Californian ruby (garnet)

117

Descriptive Names	Misnomers (and What They Really Are)
(Ruby cont.)	*Cape ruby* (garnet)
	Ruby spinel (spinel)
	Siberian ruby (tourmaline)

SAPPHIRE

Descriptive Names	Misnomers (and What They Really Are)
Australian sapphire (sapphire from Australia)	*Brazilian sapphire* (blue tourmaline. Brazil also has sapphire but they are called simply "sapphire.")
Burmese sapphire (sapphire from Burma; finest and most expensive)	*Lux sapphire* (iolite)
Ceylon sapphire (fine sapphire from Ceylon; very fine— lighter blue than Burmese)	*Water sapphire* (iolite)
Kashmir sapphire (fine sapphire from Kashmir)	
Montana sapphire (sapphire from Montana)	
Oriental sapphire (an older term that means "genuine")	
Thai sapphire (sapphire from Thailand)	

TOPAZ

Descriptive Names	Misnomers (and What They Really Are)
Precious (Imperial) topaz (usually fine apricot brown.)	*Madeira topaz* (citrine quartz)
	Occidental topaz (citrine quartz)*
	Palmeira topaz (citrine quartz)
	Rio del Sol topaz (citrine quartz)
	Rio topaz (citrine quartz)
	Saffranite topaz (citrine quartz)
	Scottish topaz (citrine quartz)
	Smokey topaz (smokey quartz)
	Spanish topaz (citrine quartz)

*Much of the citrine quartz as seen on the market today is produced by heating the purple variety (amethyst). This heating alters the color from purple to shades of yellow, yellow brown, or golden yellow.

Other Misleading Names You Might See

Names	What They Really Are
Aquagem	light blue synthetic spinel
Asparagus stone	yellow-green apatite
Beekite	fossil coral
Bengal amethyst	purple sapphire
Black amber	jet
Brazilian peridot	light green tourmaline
California moonstone	chalcedony quartz
California turquoise	variscite
Cymophane	precious cat's-eye chrysoberyl
Ebonite	vulcanized black rubber
Elbaite	pink tourmaline
Esmeralda	green tourmaline
German lapis	dyed blue jasper (quartz)
Girasol pearl	imitation pearl
Goldstone	man-made glass with copper crystals
Heliotrope	bloodstone (quartz)
Hematine	imitation hematite
Hematite garnet	iron (YIG) equivalent to YAG
Hyacinth	orange brown zircon
Imperial yu stone (*yu* is the Chinese word for jade)	fine green aventurine quartz
Jacinth	red brown zircon
Lithia amethyst	pink (kunzite)
Oriental amethyst	purple sapphire
Oriental aquamarine	aqua-colored sapphire
Oriental chrysoberyl	yellow green sapphire
Oriental topaz	yellow sapphire
Rose zircon	synthetic pink spinel
Saffronite	yellow citrine quartz
South Sea cat's-eye	operculum, door of a univalve shellfish
Swiss lapis	dyed blue jasper (quartz)

14

Buying Colored Gems

Asking the Right Questions

Is this a genuine, natural stone, or a synthetic? Synthetic stones are genuine but not natural.

Is the color natural? As opposed to irradiated, heat-treated, dyed.

What's in a name? Be particularly careful of misleading names (see page 114). When a stone is described with any qualifier, ask specifically whether or not the stone is genuine, and its color natural. Ask why a qualifier is being used.

What is the carat weight of the main stone(s)? And what is the total weight (if there is more than one stone)?

Are there any flaws, inclusions, or natural characteristics in this stone that might make it more vulnerable to breakage with normal wear? This is a particularly important question to ask when considering a colored stone. As we have mentioned, certain types of flaws or inclusions are characteristic of certain gems. An emerald *without* an inclusion would be immediately suspect, since it is so rare to encounter a flawless emerald. The existence of the flaw or inclusion isn't necessarily important, so long as it doesn't significantly mar the overall beauty or *durability* of the stone. The total number of flaws and their positioning, however, is *very* important. Any flaw that breaks the surface of the stone has weakened the stone significantly, particularly if the flaw is in a position that is normally exposed to wear—in the top, center portion of the stone. On the other hand, if the vulnerable area is on the side of the stone, protected by the setting, perhaps it may not ever pose a problem. Also, the number of flaws is important to note. Usually, a large number will detract noticeably from the beauty (especially the liveliness), but it will also generally weaken the stone and make it more susceptible to any blow or knock, and so should be avoided unless the price is right and you're willing to assume the risk.

Also, certain gems, as we've mentioned, are more brittle than others, and may break or chip more easily even without flaws. These stones include opal, zircon, and some of the new and increasingly popular gems, such as iolite (water sapphire) and tanzanite. This does not mean you should avoid buying them, but it does mean you should give thought to how they will be worn—ring? bracelet? brooch? pendant? earrings?—and how frequently. Rings and bracelets are particularly vulnerable, since they are more susceptible to blows or knocks; brooches, pendants, and earrings are less vulnerable. But you may still want to consider, for example, a tanzanite ring if it will be worn only occasionally or in situations where care is easy to exercise, such as evening wear. We could never recommend a tanzanite ring for all-day, everyday wear—the risk of damage would be too great.

Another consideration should be permanence of color. For some inexplicable reason, the color in certain stones seems prone to fading. Two examples are amethyst and kunzite (one of the new and increasingly popular gems). Just which ones will and which ones won't, and over how long, no one can know. This phenomenon has never affected the popularity of amethyst and we see no reason for it to affect kunzite's popularity, but we feel the consumer should be aware of it. And perhaps some protection from too much exposure to strong sunlight, or usage restricted to evening wear, would be wise to consider.

Also, the setting may be of special importance when considering one of these stones. A tanzanite, opal, or emerald set in a ring must be designed to provide protection (for example, by surrounding the major stone with diamonds). A design in which the stone is unusually exposed, such as in a high setting or one with open, unprotected sides, would be most undesirable.

Do you feel this is a well-cut stone? This is an important question to ask if the stone seems dull or lifeless, even after cleaning. If this is the case, ask if the jeweler has something that is cut better and exhibits a little more brilliance. Now you can compare it in terms of what you like and what you can afford. Remember, however, that if a colored stone (especially pastel shades) is cut too shallow (flat), it will lose its appeal quickly because of the accumulation of grease and dirt on the back. This can be immediately remedied by a good cleaning.

What are these colorless stones? In a piece of jewelry where a colored main stone is surrounded by colorless stones to accentuate it or highlight its color, ask, "What are the colorless stones?" Do not assume they are diamonds. They may be diamonds, zircons, man-made diamond simulations such as CZ or YAG, or synthetic white spinel. (Spinel is the most frequently used in the Orient.)

Information That Should Be Included in the Bill of Sale

Always make sure that any item you purchase is clearly described in the bill of sale as represented to you by the salesman or jeweler. Essential information includes the following:

1. Whether or not the stone(s) is genuine or synthetic, and not in any way a composite (doublet, triplet).
2. That the color is natural if it has been so represented.
3. A statement describing the overall color (hue, tone, and intensity).
4. A statement describing the overall flaw picture. (This is not always necessary with colored stones. In the case of a flawless or nearly flawless stone it is wise to note the excellent clarity. Note any unusual flaw that might prove useful for identification.)
5. A statement describing the cut or make. (This is not always necessary, but may be useful if it is especially well cut, or an unusual or fancy cut).
6. The carat weight of the main stone(s) plus total weight if there is a combination of main stone(s) and smaller stones.
7. If the piece is being represented as being made by a famous designer or house (Van Cleef and Arpels, Tiffany, Caldwell) and the price reflects this claim, the claim should be warranted on the bill of sale and the location of the mark of said designer or house should be indicated.

8. If the piece is being represented as antique (technically, an antique must be at least 100 years old) and you are paying a premium for its age, the period should be stated on the bill of sale: "dating from approximately 1850," etc.

9. If the stone (piece) is to be taken on approval, make sure millimeter dimensions—top to bottom, as well as length, width, or diameter—are provided, as well as a full description of the stone or piece. Also, make sure a time period is indicated, such as "2 days," and make sure before you sign anything that you are signing an approval form and *not* a binding contract for its purchase.

Special Tips to Remember When Buying a Colored Stone

Ask the jeweler to clean the stone to remove dirt and grease or color enhancers before you examine it. Due to the more fragile quality of many colored stones, it is wise *not* to use an ultrasonic cleaner for colored stones. (This may be the jeweler's worry if it's his stone; but if he offers to clean your lovely ring, etc., keep this in mind.)

When looking at unmounted stones, *look at them through the side as well as from the top.* Look for evenness of color versus color zoning—shades of lighter or darker color creating streaks or planes of differing color.

Remember to give special attention to wearability. If you are considering one of the more fragile stones, think about how the piece will be worn, where, and how frequently. Also, pay special attention to the setting and whether it is set in a way that will add protection, or allow unnecessary, risky exposure to hazards.

Get the facts on the bill of sale.

If a stone is an expensive 1 carat or larger, make the sale contingent upon verification of the facts by a qualified gemologist, appraiser, or gem-testing lab such as GIA, IGL, or AGL.

Remember that color is the most important consideration, followed by cut and proportion. The presence of flaws or inclusions doesn't detract from the stone's value as significantly as with diamonds. (If the overall color or beauty is not seriously affected, the presence of flaws should not deter a purchase. But, conversely, flawless stones may bring a disproportionately higher price per carat due to their rarity, and larger sizes will also command higher prices.)

Ornamental Gems

Some gems are not transparent; you can't see through them clearly. Let's note very briefly the following terms, which will frequently be used in describing these.

Terms Used to Describe Ornamental Gems

Transparent. Light travels through the stone easily, with minimal distortion, enabling one to see through it easily.

Translucent. It transmits light but diffuses it, creating an effect like frosted glass. If one tries to read print through such a stone, the print will appear as a darkened area, and the print outline will be obscured.

Opaque. Transmits *no* light. One cannot see through it even at a thin edge.

Special Optical Effects

Adularescence. A billowy, movable, colored cloud effect seen in some stones, such as moonstone; an internal, movable sheen.

Asterism. Used to describe the display of a star effect (four- or 6-rayed) seen when a stone is cut in a cabochon style (star ruby, garnet, and sapphire.)

Chatoyancy. The effect produced in some stones (when cut in a cabochon style) of a thin, bright line across the stone (which usually moves as the stone is moved from side to side), sometimes called a cat's-eye effect.

Iridescence. A rainbow color effect produced by a thin film of air or liquid within the stone. Most iridescence seen in stones is the result of a crack breaking its surface. This detracts from the value, even if it looks pretty.

Luster. Usually refers to the surface of a stone and the degree to which it reflects light. Seen as the shine on the stone. Diamond, for example, has much greater luster than amethyst. Pearls are also evaluated for their luster, but pearls have a softer, silkier-looking reflection than other gems. The luster in pearls is often called orient.

Play of color. Used frequently to describe the fire seen in opal.

Cut

Cabochon. A facetless style of cutting that produces smooth, round, convex surfaces. Usually oval, round, or navette (boat-shaped).

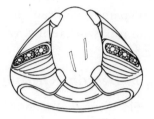

Cabochon cut

Faceted. A style of cutting that consists of giving to the stone many small faces at varying angles to one another, as in various diamond cuts. The placement, angle, and shape of the faces, or facets, is carefully planned and executed to bring out the stone's inherent beauty—fire, color, brilliance—to the fullest.

Guides to Popular Gems

The following charts show what stones are available in various colors and their wearability, price, and availability. Chapters 15 and 16 describe the stones (listed by family), and provide important information particular to each.

Note that prices quoted are for faceted gemstones. Cabochon-cut stones usually cost much less. Also, prices are for "fair" to "very fine" quality. Exceptionally fine, rare stones, or stones of rare size and quality, can sell for much more than prices indicated here.

Now you will know what to ask the jeweler to show you—and don't forget to do a lot of window-shopping, looking and asking questions, until you really have developed a feel for that particular stone and the market for it.

GEM ALTERNATIVES BY COLOR

Color Family	Popular Name of Stone	Gem Family
Red—*from red to shades of pink*	*Ruby*—red bluish red to orange red	Corundum
	Garnet—several red color varieties	Garnet
	Pyrope—brownish red to red	Garnet
	Almandine—violet to pure red	Garnet
	Spessartite—orange red to reddish brown to brownish red	Garnet
	Rhodolite—red to violet	Garnet
	Spinel—red to brownish red and pink	Spinel
	Pink sapphire—pinkish red	Corundum
	Zircon—brownish red to deep, dark red	Zircon
	Scapolite—light red	Scapolite
	Rubellite—red to violet red and pink	Tourmaline
	Morganite—pink to orange pink	Beryl
	Kunzite—violet pink to pink violet	Spodumene
	Rose quartz—pure pink	Quartz
	Andalusite—pink to reddish brown	Andalusite
Orange	*Padparadsha sapphire*—pinkish orange	Corundum
	Scapolite—orange	Scapolite
	Topaz—brownish orange and yellow orange	Topaz
	Spinel—brown to orange	Spinel
	Zircon—orange to golden brown	Zircon
	Hessonite—orange brown	Garnet
	Malaya—pink orange to brownish red	Garnet
	Tourmaline—orangy brown, yellow orange	Tourmaline
	Beryl—orange	Beryl

Color Family	Popular Name of Stone	Gem Family
Yellow	*Scapolite*—yellow	Scapolite
	Sapphire—yellow	Corundum
	Beryl—golden yellow	Beryl
	Sphene—green yellow to golden yellow to brown	Sphene
	Chrysoberyl—yellow, yellow green, yellow brown	Chrysoberyl
	Citrine—yellow to yellow brown	Quartz
	Grossularite—yellow to yellowish green to yellowish brown	Garnet
	Zircon—yellow to yellow brown	Zircon
Green	*Emerald*—yellowish green to bluish green	Beryl
	Tsavorite—yellowish green to bluish green	Garnet
	Sphene—grass green to yellow green	Sphene
	Tourmaline—all shades of green	Tourmaline
	Peridot—yellow green to green	Peridot
	Zircon—green to yellow green to gray green	Zircon
	Alexandrite—daylight: bluish to blue green; artificial light: violet red	Chrysoberyl
	Sapphire—yellow green to blue green to gray green	Corundum
	Scapolite—greenish gray	Scapolite
	Demantoid—yellow green to emerald green	Garnet
Blue	*Sapphire*—cornflower blue to greenish blue to inky blue	Corundum
	Tanzanite—violet blue	Zoisite
	Spinel—gray blue, greenish blue, true pastel blue	Spinel
	Aquamarine—pastel to deep blue to blue green	Beryl
	Indicolite—inky blue, greenish blue	Tourmaline
	Topaz—pastel to dark blue to blue green	Topaz
	Zircon—pastel blue	Zircon
	Water sapphire—violet blue	Iolite

128

Color Family	Popular Name of Stone	Gem Family
Violet	*Scapolite*—violet blue to greenish to bluish gray, lilac to violet	Scapolite
	Amethyst—lilac to violet to reddish purple to brownish purple	Quartz
	Sapphire—purple to violet	Corundum
	Rhodolite—red violet	Garnet
	Spinel—grayish violet to pure purple	Spinel
	Morganite—lavender	Beryl

GUIDE TO POPULAR GEMS AND THEIR PRICES

FAMILY	POPULAR NAME	COLOR(S)	APPROX. RETAIL COST PER CARAT JULY 1987	BRIILLIANCE	WEAR-ABILITY	AVAILA-BILITY
Andalusite	"Poor man's alexandrite"	Changes color from grayish green to reddish brown, emerald green to bright yellow	1-5 ct: $80-$400 6-10 ct: $120-$600	Good	Good	Large: scarce Smaller: fair
Beryl[1]	Aquamarine	Pastel blue to medium deep blue	5-15 ct: $175-$1,500	Good	Good	Good
	Golden beryl (Heliodor)	Yellow; brownish yellow	5-10 ct: $90-$250 10-20 ct: $100-$700	Good	Good	Good
	Emerald	Yellow green to blue green	1-5 ct, medium quality: $3,600-$14,000	Fair to good	Fair to good	Very fine Colombian, rare; Others, good
	Morganite	Pink to orange pink	5-10 ct: $100-$575	Good	Good	Fine: rare Medium: good
Chrysoberyl	Alexandrite	Changes from greenish in daylight to reddish in incandescent light	1-2 ct: $2,400-$9,500 3-5 ct: $7,000-$25,000 6-10 ct: $10,000-$35,000	Good	Excellent	Large: scarce Small: fair
	Chrysoberyl	Yellow to yellow brown to yellow green	1-5 ct: $70-$250 5-10 ct: $150-$650	Good	Excellent	Fair
	Precious cat's-eye	Greenish to brownish yellow with "eye" effect	3-5 ct: $1,200-$5,000 6-10 ct: $1,800-$6,500	Negligible	Excellent	Fair to good
Corundum	Ruby	Red to bluish or purplish red to yellow red	medium-good-quality: 1-2 ct: $2,000-$12,000 3-4 ct: $4,000-$20,000 5-8 ct: $8,000-$45,000[2]	Fair to good	Excellent	Burmese: rare Thai: good Kenya: fair Ceylon: good

	Variety	Color	Price			Availability
(Corundum cont.)	Blue sapphire	Bright blue to inky blue	1-2 ct: $100-$6,000 3-4 ct: $200-$16,000 5-6 ct: $700-$20,000	Good	Excellent	Kashmir: scarce Burmese: scarce Thai: good Australian: good
	Colorless sapphire	White (colorless)	under 1 ct: $30-$60 1-1.5 ct: $50-$100	Good	Very good	Good in sizes under 1 ct
	Green sapphire	Clear green to brownish or bluish green	1-4 ct: $40-$200 5-10 ct: $125-$300	Good	Excellent	Large: scarce Others: fair
	Pink sapphire	Light to very dark pink (almost red)	1 ct: $100-$6,000 2 ct: $375-$12,000 3 ct: $500-$16,000	Good	Excellent	Fair
	Yellow sapphire	Yellow (most are heat treated; natural yellow usually less brilliant).	1-5 ct: $100-$1,600 5-10 ct: $150-$2,500	Good	Excellent	Good
Garnet	Almandine (common garnet)	Violet to pure red	1-3 ct: $10-$100 4-6 ct: $20-$125	Fair to good	Good	Good
	Demantoid	Yellow green to emerald green	1-2 ct: $800-$8,000 3-4 ct: $2,000-$12,000	Very good	Good	Poor
	Grossularite	Yellowish to yellowish green to yellowish brown	1-3 ct: $50-$165 4-6 ct: $120-$325	Fair to good	Good	Good
	Malaya	Pink orange to brownish red	5-10 ct: $200-$750	Good	Good	Good
	Pyrope (common garnet)	Yellowish red to dark red	1-5 ct: $30-$100	Fair to good	Good	Good
	Rhodolite	Red violet	6-12 ct: $75-$200 1-5 ct: $30-$200	Good	Good	Good
	Spessartite	Brownish orange to reddish brown to brownish red	5-10 ct: $100-$450 1-5 ct: $50-$300	Good	Good	Fair
	Tsavorite	Yellowish green to bluish green	5-10 ct: $100-$350 1-5 ct: $800-$4,000 5-10 ct: $1,800-$8,000	Good	Good	Over 5 cts. scarce; other sizes fair to good

(Price Charts continued on next page)

FAMILY	POPULAR NAME	COLOR(S)	APPROX. RETAIL COST PER CARAT JULY 1987	BRILLIANCE	WEAR-ABILITY	AVAILABILITY
Iolite	Water sapphire	Violet blue	1-5 ct: $25-$125 5-10 ct: $60-$350	Good	Fair	Good
Pearls (cultured)[3]	Round[4]	Silver, silver white, pink white, white, cream	Matched pairs:[5] 7½ mm: $40-$250 8½ mm: $300-$1,000 9½ mm: $450-$3,000 16" strand—uniform: 6½ mm: $600-$1,950 7½ mm: $900-$4,500 8½ mm: $1,200-$12,800 9½ mm: $3,000-$36,000	n.a.	Good	Gem quality over 8 mm: rare Others: good
	South Sea (round)	Silver, silver white, pink white, white, cream	16" strand—graduated: 10-14½ mm: $15-$150,000 11-16 mm: $25-$250,000	n.a.	Good	Gem quality: very rare Fine quality over 16 mm: rare Others: fair-good.
	Baroque	White to creamy white	16" strand—uniform: 7-8 mm: $450-$1,000 8-9 mm: $900-$1,800	n.a.	Good	Good
	Freshwater	All colors	16" strand: Rice shaped 4-5 mm: $40-$180 6-7 mm: $140-$450 Flat 4-5 mm: $120-$225 6-7 mm: $140-$450	n.a.	Good	Good

		Color	Price			
Pearls Black/Gray (cultured)			Biwa rice 4-5 mm: $350 (fine) 5-6 mm: $600 (fine) Biwa flat 4-5 mm: $400 (fine) 5-6 mm: $675 (fine)			
	Round	Dyed gray	16" strand—uniform: 5-6 mm: $900 7-8 mm: $2,200 8-9 mm: $3,500	n.a.	Good	Good (*natural* gray color rare; much more expensive than dyed)
	Baroque	Dyed gray	16" strand—uniform: 5-6 mm: $500 7-8 mm: $1,400 8-9 mm: $2,200	n.a.	Good	Good (*natural* color gray rare; much more expensive than dyed)
	Round	Dyed or irradiated black/blue	16" strand: 5-6 mm: $800 7-8 mm: $2,000 8-9 mm: $3,000	n.a.	Good	Good (*natural* black color very rare; much more expensive)
	Baroque	Dyed or irradiated black/blue	16" strand—uniform: 5-6 mm: $350 7-8 mm: $900 8-9 mm: $1,500	n.a.	Good	Good
Peridot	Peridot	Yellow green to deep green to rich chartreuse	1-5 ct: $30-$225 6-15 ct: $60-$500	Fair to good	Fair—will scratch easily	Large: scarce Smaller: plentiful
Quartz	Amethyst	Purple, reddish purple to brownish purple	1-5 ct: $8-$75 5-10 ct: $12-$90 10-20 ct: $15-$120	Fair to good	Good	Very good
	Citrine	Yellow to yellow brown	1-5 ct: $4-$40 5-10 ct: $6-$50	Good	Good	Good
	Rose quartz	Pure pink; some murky; some clear, transparent	1-5 cts: $5-$10 for clear; under $2 for murky	Good	Good	Good

(Price Charts continued on next page)

133

FAMILY	POPULAR NAME	COLOR(S)	APPROX. RETAIL COST PER CARAT JULY 1987	BRILLIANCE	WEAR-ABILITY	AVAILA-BILITY
(Quartz cont.)	(Rose quartz cont.) Smokey	Brown shades	5-15 cts: up to $30 for clear 1-20ct: $1.00-$2.00	Good	Good	Very good
Spinel	Red spinel	Red to brownish red	Ruby red, 1-3 ct: $2,400-$4,500 All other reds, 1-10 ct: $400-$2,200	Very good	Very good	Ruby red: scarce Others: good
	Pink spinel	Lively or bright pink to brownish pink	1-5 ct: $100-$1,500	Very good	Very good	Fair
	Blue spinel	Medium gray blue to deep blue to violet	1-5 ct: $50-$400	Good	Very good	Good
Spodumene	Kunzite	Lilac, violet, pink	1-10 ct: $10-$140 10-20 ct: $50-$300	Good	Poor for rings	Very good
Topaz[6]	Blue Topaz	Blue	1-5 cts: $16-$75 5-10 cts: $20-$75	Good	Fair	Good
	Pink Topaz	Pink (red also available, but very rare and much more expensive)	1-3 ct: $80-$400 4-6 ct: $120-$750 10-15 ct: $150-$1,000	Good	Fair	Fair to good
	Imperial	Golden with pinkish/reddish overtone	1-5 ct: $90-$950 6-10 ct: $180-$1,400	Good	Fair	Fair to good except in very large sizes
	Yellow Topaz	Yellow/golden (no pink/red overtone)	1-5 ct: $45-$475 5-10 ct: $60-$550	Good	Good	Good
Tourmaline	Chrome	Deep green	1-3 ct: $120-$800 4-6 ct: $200-$1,000 8-10 ct: $300-$1,800	Good	Fair to good	Scarce
	Indicolite	Inky blue to blue green	1-3 ct: $50-$900 4-6 ct: $90-$1,200	Good	Fair to good	Good

	Color	Price			
Pink	Pink or rose	10–20 ct: $200–$1,600 1–3 ct: $40–$300 4–6 ct: $60–$400 7–10 ct: $80–$575	Good	Fair to good	Good
Rubellite	Red to red violet	1–3 ct: $50–$600 3–5 ct: $150–$800 6–8 ct: $300–$1,200 10–20 ct: $600–$1,800	Good	Fair to good	Good
Verdelite	Green—all shades except chrome tourmaline	1–3 ct: $40–$300 4–6 ct: $60–$400 10–20 ct: $200–$750	Good	Fair to good	Good
Bicolor and tricolor	Yellow, orange, and brown varieties	1–5 ct: $40–$300	Good	Fair to good	Fair
	Red/black, red/green, red/green/colorless	1–5 ct: $50–$600 6–10 ct: $100–$900	Good	Fair to good	Good
Zircon	Pastel blue (usually heat-treated)	1–3 ct: $40–$175 4–6 ct: $70–$350 7–10 ct: $100–$500	Good	Fair—not recommended for rings	Large: scarce
	Green to yellow green	1–3 ct: $35–$175 4–6 ct: $65–$200 7–10 ct: $100–$350	Good	Fair—not recommended for rings	Good
	Colorless (usually heat-treated)	1–3 ct: $30–$90 4–6 ct: $60–$180 7–10 ct: $80–$300	Good	Fair—not recommended for rings	Good
	Orange to golden brown	Comparable to green	Good	Fair—not recommended for rings	Good
	Red to brownish red	Comparable to blue	Good	Fair—not recommended for rings	True red: scarce Other reds: good
	Yellow to yellow brown	Comparable to green	Good	Fair—not recommended for rings	Good

(Price Charts continued on next page)

135

FAMILY	POPULAR NAME	COLOR(S)	APPROX. RETAIL COST PER CARAT JULY 1987	BRILLIANCE	WEAR-ABILITY	AVAILA-BILITY
Zoisite	Tanzanite	Strong blue to weak violet, blue violet	1-3 ct: $350-$2,000 4-6 ct: $600-$2,600 10-15 ct: $800-$4,600	Good	Poor for rings	Fair

[1]Beryl also comes in red, green (different from emerald green), lilac, salmon, and orange. Most are still not easily available, but some, such as the lovely orange variety, can be found for under $75. a carat and offer excellent value.

[2]Cabochon-cut rubies, sapphires and emeralds usually cost much less; finest gems can cost much more.

[3]Natural pearls are very rare and much more expensive than cultured. Pricing information is insufficient to provide guidelines.

[4]3/4 *round* pearls which may *appear* to be fully round, sell for approximately *50% less* than full round pearls.

[5]Fully drilled pearls mounted on a gold "post" sell for much less than undrilled pearls.

[6]Topaz enhanced by heating and/or radiation costs much less.

136

15

Precious Gemstones

Emerald

Emerald is the green variety of the mineral beryl and one of the most highly prized of all the gems. Aside from being the birthstone for May, it was historically believed to bestow on its wearer faithfulness and unchanging love, and was thought to enable the wearer to forecast events.

The finest-quality emerald has the color of fresh young green grass—an almost pure spectral green, possibly with a very faint tint of blue, as in the "drop of oil" emerald from Colombia, which is considered to be the world's finest. Flawless emeralds are rare, so the flaws have come to serve almost as "fingerprints," while flawless emeralds are immediately suspect. Although a hard stone, emerald will chip easily since it tends to be somewhat brittle, so special care should be given in wearing and handling.

Because of emerald's popularity and value, imitations are abundant. Glass (manufactured complete with "flaws"), doublets or triplets—such as "aquamarine emeralds" and "Tecla emeralds," which are clever imitations made by inserting layers of green glass (or, more frequently, a green cementing agent) between pieces of aquamarine or quartz "crystal"—are often encountered. Also, fine synthetic emer-

137

alds have been produced for many years with nearly the same physical and optical properties (color, hardness, brilliance) as genuine emerald. These synthetics are not inexpensive themselves, except by comparison to a genuine emerald of equivalent quality.

Techniques to enhance color and reduce the visibility of flaws are also frequently used. A common practice is to boil the emerald in oil (sometimes tinted green), a practice that goes back to early Greek times. This is a widely accepted trade practice, since it is actually good for the stone in light of its fragile nature. Oiling hides some of the whitish flaws, which are actually cracks, filling the cracks so they become less visible. The oil becomes an integral part of the emerald unless it is subjected to some type of degreasing procedure. The development and use of the ultrasonic cleaner has brought to light the extensiveness of this practice. Never clean emeralds in an ultrasonic cleaner.

A good friend of mine took her heirloom emerald ring to her jeweler for a "really good cleaning." Luckily for the jeweler, she never left the store and was standing right there when the ring was put into the cleaner and removed. She couldn't believe her eyes. She was shocked by the loss of color and the "sudden appearance of more flaws." The ultrasonic cleaner had removed the oil that had penetrated the cracks, and an emerald several shades lighter and more visibly flawed emerged. Had she not been there, she would never have believed the jeweler hadn't pulled a switch.

Oiling is considered an acceptable practice, but be sure the price reflects the actual quality of the stone.

As with all highly desired gems, the greater the value and demand, the greater the occurrence of fraudulent practices. Examples of almost every type of technique to simulate emerald can be found—color alteration (using green foil on closed backs), synthetics, substitutes (less valuable green stones), doublets or other composites, etc. Therefore, be especially cautious of bargains, deal with reputable jewelers when planning to purchase, and always have the purchase double-checked by a qualified gemologist-appraiser.

Ruby

Prized through the ages, even by kings, as the "gem of gems ... surpassing all other precious stones in virtue," and today's birthstone for July, ruby is the red variety of the mineral corundum. Historically, it has been symbolic of love and passion, considered to be an aid to firm friendship, and believed to ensure beauty. Its color ranges from purplish or bluish red to a yellowish red. The finest color is a vivid, almost pure spectral red with a very faint undertone of blue, as seen in Burmese rubies, which are considered the finest. The ruby is a very brilliant stone and is also a very hard, durable, and wearable stone (a hardness of 9 on Mohs' scale). Because of these characteristics, ruby makes an unusually fine choice for any piece of jewelry.

Translucent varieties of ruby are also seen, and one variety exhibits a six-ray star effect when cut as a cabochon. This variety is called star ruby and is one of nature's most beautiful and interesting gifts to man. But, as with so many other beautiful gifts once produced only in nature, today man has also learned to make synthetic star ruby.

Here again, remember that the greater the value and demand, the greater the use of techniques to "improve" or to simulate. Again, examples of almost every type of technique can be found—color enhancement, synthesis, substitutes, doublets, triplets, misleading names, etc. The newest synthetic rubies—the Kashan ruby and Chatham ruby—are so close to natural ruby in every aspect that many are actually passing for genuine, even among many gemologists. When getting a very fine, valuable ruby certified, make every effort to select a gemologist with both many years' experience in colored gems and an astute knowledge of the marketplace today.

Here again, be especially cautious of bargains. Deal with reputable jewelers when planning to purchase, and have the purchase double-checked by a qualified gemologist-appraiser.

Sapphire

The "celestial" sapphire, symbol of the heavens, bestower of innocence, truth, good health, and preserver of chastity, is reserved today as the birthstone of September. Sapphire is corundum. While we know it best in its blue variety, which is one of the most highly prized varieties, it comes in essentially every color (the red variety is ruby). As we mentioned when discussing ruby, sapphire's hardness, brilliance, and availability in so many beautiful colors make it probably the most important and most versatile of the gem families.

The finest sapphires are considered to be the blue variety—specifically those from Burma and Kashmir, which are closest to the pure spectral blue. Fine, brilliant, deep blue Burmese sapphires will surely dazzle the eye and the pocketbook, as will the Kashmir, which is a fine velvety-toned deep blue. Many today tend to be too dark, however, because of the presence of too much black and poor cutting (cutting deep for additional weight), but the deep blues can be treated to lighten the color.

The Ceylon sapphires are a very pleasing shade of blue, but are a less deep shade than the Burmese or Kashmir, often on the pastel side.

We are also seeing many Australian sapphires. These are often a dark blue, but have a slightly green undertone, as do those from Thailand, and sell for much less per carat. They offer a very affordable alternative to the Burmese, Kashmir, or Ceylon, and can still be very pleasing in their color. Blue sapphires also come from Tanzania, Brazil, Africa, and even the U.S.A. (Montana and North Carolina).

With sapphire, origin can have a significant effect on price, so if you are purchasing a Burmese or Ceylon sapphire, that should be noted on the bill of sale.

Like ruby, the blue sapphire may be found in a translucent variety that may show a six-rayed star effect when cut into a cabochon. This variety is known as star sapphire, of which there are numerous synthetics (often referred to in the trade as "Lindea" (pronounced Lin'dee).

In addition to blue sapphire, we are now beginning to see the appearance of many other color varieties in the latest jewelry designs—especially yellow and pink, and in smaller sizes some beautiful shades of green. These are known as fancy sapphires. Compared to the cost of blue sapphire and ruby, these stones offer excellent value and real beauty. These are gems to watch for in the future.

Inevitably, one can find evidence of every technique known to improve the perceived quality and value of the sapphire—the alteration of color, synthesis, composites, misleading names. Techniques have been developed to treat natural sapphires to remove a certain type of flaw (needle type) and to change the color—for example, to create a "Ceylon" sapphire that never came from Ceylon (Sri Lanka) but whose color looks like that of a Ceylon. Yet again, we urge you to be especially cautious of bargains, deal with reputable jewelers, and have your stone double-checked by a qualified gemologist-appraiser.

Oriental Pearls

June's birthstone, the pearl, pure and fair to the eye, has been recognized since the earliest times as the emblem of modesty, chastity, and purity.

A fine natural or Oriental pearl—the real "genuine pearl"—is considered a precious gem, since they are relatively rare in nice sizes today. The pearl business is almost entirely in the cultured pearl market.

Pearls are produced by oysters (not the edible variety) in saltwater and by mussels in freshwater lakes and rivers. They produce the pearl nacre naturally, and it takes years to produce a fine, large pearl. As with all things, quality and value vary.

The quality and value of the genuine natural pearl are determined by:

- Freedom from skin blemishes (blisters, pimples, or spots).
- Roundness—the more perfectly round the better.
- Luster—the higher the luster the better (luster may be called *Orient* by some gemologists).
- Tint—rose-tinted pearls are considered the most valuable, although there are also white and cream colored pearls that are highly desirable.
- Size—*Oriental pearls* (natural) are sold by weight. Pearls are weighed as "grains"—4 grains equal 1 carat. *Cultured pearls* are measured in millimeters. The larger the pearl, the greater the cost, jumping dramatically, for example, between 7½ mm and 8 mm, which is considered large; or between 9 and 10 mm, which is very large both in size and in price. The price jumps upward rapidly with each millimeter once you pass 8 mm.

A fine pearl necklace, or any strung pearl item, requires very careful matching of size, roundness, luster, tint, and skin texture. Graduated pearls—a strand containing larger pearls in the center, with the pearls becoming progressively smaller toward the ends—also require careful sizing. Failure to match carefully will detract from both the appearance of the piece and the value.

Pearls should be handled with care. It is best to keep them in a separate pouch, and to exercise some caution when wearing to avoid contact with certain substances such as vinegar (when making a salad), ammonia, inks, and certain perfumes, since these can spot the pearl's surface. Also, the frequent application of hair spray while wearing pearls will coat them and make them very dull, but this coating can be cleaned by washing in nail polish remover.

The Pearl Market Today Is a Cultured Pearl Market

When we speak of pearls today we are usually referring to cultured, or cultivated, pearls. The cost of fine cultured pearls has become very high and continues to rise.

Cultured pearls are usually produced by inserting a mother-of-pearl bead into the mantle (tissue) of a live oyster and then returning it to the water. Over time (usually several years), the oyster secretes a coating of nacre over it, a coating rarely thicker than ½ mm. The thickness depends in part upon the length of time the bead remains in the oyster. Sometimes the cultured pearl is removed from the oyster prematurely, so that the nacre coating is too thin and may begin to wear through in only a few years. In other cases, the cultured pearl is so fine as to require an expert to tell it from a fine, genuine natural pearl.

In terms of quality and value, the same factors are used to determine the quality and value of a cultured pearl as for a natural pearl. But a pearl must always be clearly described as cultured or genuine (Oriental), and this should be stated in writing on your bill of sale since Oriental pearls are much more costly than cultured pearls.

A Word About Biwa And Other Freshwater Pearls

Biwa pearls are grown in fresh water (lakes and rivers) and derive their name from Lake Biwa in Japan, where very fine freshwater pearls are grown. Until recently, the term "Biwa" was often used for any freshwater pearl. Today it is used only for those from Lake Biwa.

Freshwater pearls are grown in many countries including the United States, China and Ireland. Common mussel-type molluscs are used. The process does not require the insertion of a mother-of-pearl bead, so the pearls grow much faster and each mussel can simultaneously produce many pearls (unlike the saltwater oyster, which normally produces only a single pearl). As a result, most freshwater pearls are much less expensive than saltwater pearls.

The most familiar freshwater pearls have long, narrow, rice-shaped outlines. They can also be round, but these are rare and expensive. They can be smooth or wrinkled and come in many lovely colors.

A Word About Baroque Pearls

Baroque pearls are both genuine (natural) and cultured. Their shape is more or less irregular, but they are distinctive because of their very beautiful tints of color. Their irregular shape renders them far less valuable than round pearls. Nonetheless, they make beautiful, versatile fashion accessories.

Is the Color Natural?

Cultured pearls are available in many colors—gray, black, pink, blue—but often these colors have been produced by surface dyes. White pearls that have been tinted and then drilled for jewelry use (as in a necklace) can be easily detected by a qualified gemologist.

Is It Real or Simulated?

Simulated or imitation pearls are sold everywhere. Many of the finest imitations have been mistaken for fine cultured pearls. One test is to run the pearl gently between your teeth. The cultured or genuine pearl will have a mildly abrasive or gritty feel, while the imitation will be slippery smooth. (This test won't work with false teeth.) Try the test on pearls you know are cultured or genuine, and then try it on known imitations to get a feel for the difference.

But once again, when in doubt, seek out a qualified gemologist. The cost may be too great to risk it.

A Final Word

There are innumerable differences in quality—if roundness is good, luster may be poor; if luster is good, roundness may be poor; if color and luster are good, there may be poor surface texture from too many skin blemishes, or matching in a strand may be poor. Shopping around can teach you a tremendous amount about pearls. Keeping in mind the factors that affect quality—size, luster, color, roundness, skin blemishes—go window-shopping and compare. You may find you like a certain color or luster but can't afford a strand of 8-mm pearls, but would be just as happy with 7½ mm, which are considerably cheaper.

16

Other Colored Gems

Alexandrite

Alexandrite is a fascinating transparent gem that appears grass green in daylight and raspberry red under artificial light. It is a variety of chrysoberyl reputedly discovered in Russia in 1831 on the day Alexander II reached his majority; hence the name. In Russia, where the national colors also happen to be green and red, it is considered a stone of very good omen. It is also considered Friday's stone or the stone of "Friday's child." Alexandrite is a relatively recent gem. Nonetheless, it has definitely come into its own and is presently commanding both high interest and high prices. While not too uncommon in small sizes, it has become relatively scarce in sizes of 2 carats or more. A fine 3-carat stone can cost $20,000 today. If you see an alexandrite that measures more than ½ inch in width, you can be sure it is a fake. Alexandrite is normally cut in a faceted style, but some cat's-eye type alexandrites, found in Brazil, would be cut as a cabochon to display the eye effect. These are usually small; the largest we've seen was approximately 3 carats.

Prior to 1973, there were really no good synthetic alexandrites. While some varieties of synthetic corundum and synthetic spinel were frequently sold as alexandrite, they really didn't look like the

145

real thing but were hard to differentiate from the real thing since so few had ever seen the real thing. They are, however, easy for a gemologist to spot. In 1973 a very good synthetic alexandrite was produced, which is not easy to differentiate from the real thing. While a good gemologist today can tell the synthetic from the genuine, when they first appeared on the market many were mistaken for the real thing. So today be especially careful to verify the authenticity of your alexandrite, since it might have been mistakenly identified years ago, and passed along as the real thing to you today. It could save you a lot of money!

Amber

Amber is not a stone, but rather an amorphous, fossilized tree sap. It was one of the early substances used by man for decoration. Modestly decorated pieces of rough amber have been found in Stone Age excavations and are assumed to have been used as amulets and talismans—a use definitely recorded throughout history before, during, and since the ancient Greeks. Because of its beautiful color and the ease with which it could be fashioned, amber quickly became a favorite object of trade and barter and personal adornment.

It varies from transparent to semitranslucent, and from yellow to dark brown in color; occasionally it's seen in reddish and greenish brown tones. In addition, amber is dyed many colors. Occasionally, one can find "foreign" fragments or insects that were trapped in the amber (which usually adds to its value because of the added curiosity factor).

Plastics are the most common amber imitations. But real amber (which is the lightest gem material) may be easily distinguished from most plastic when dropped into a saturated salt solution—amber will float while most plastic sinks. One other commonly encountered "amber" type is "reconstructed" amber—amber fragments compressed under heat to form a larger piece. An expert can differentiate this from the real under magnification.

Amber can be easily tested by touching it in an inconspicuous place with a hot needle (held by tweezers). The whitish smoke that should be produced should smell like burning pine wood, not like medicine or disinfectant. If there is no smoke, but a black mark occurs, then it is *not* amber. Another test is to try to cut a little piece of the amber with a sharp pointed knife, at the drill hole of the bead; if it cuts like wood (producing a shaving), it is *not* amber, which would produce a sharp, crumbly deposit.

With the exception of those pieces possessing special antique value, the value of amber fluctuates with its popularity, which in part is dictated by the fashion industry and the prevalence of yellow and browns in one's wardrobe. Nonetheless, amber has proved itself an ageless gem and will always be loved and admired.

Amethyst

Amethyst, a transparent purple variety of quartz, is one of the most popular of the colored stones. In contemporary times, recognized as the birthstone of February, it was once believed to bring peace of mind to the wearer. It was also believed to prevent the wearer from getting drunk, and if the circle of the sun or moon was engraved thereon, it was believed to prevent death from poison.

Available in shades from light to dark purple, it is relatively hard, fairly brilliant, and overall a good, versatile, wearable stone, available in good supply even in very large sizes (although large sizes with deep color are now becoming scarce). Amethyst is probably one of the most beautiful stones available at a moderate price, although one must be careful because "fine" amethyst is being produced synthetically today. It frequently exhibits color zoning (often looking like chevrons).

Amethyst may fade from heat and strong sunshine. Guard your amethyst from these conditions and it will retain its color indefinitely.

Andalusite (Poor Man's Alexandrite)

Andalusite is now offering interesting new possibilities for jewelry. Brazil is the primary source of these fascinating, fairly hard, and fairly durable stones. While it is not the world's most beautiful stone, nor the world's most readily available yet, it may be one of its most interesting, due to the several colors it may exhibit—an olive green in one direction, a rich reddish brown from another direction, and grayish green from yet another direction. In an emerald cut it may look primarily green while exhibiting an orange color at the ends of emerald shape. In a round cut you may see the green body color with simultaneous flashes of another color. And one benefit it has over alexandrite is that you don't have to change the light in which it is being seen to experience its colors. There is also an emerald green variety that may exhibit a bright yellow simultaneously, or when viewed from different angles (this is a rarer and somewhat more expensive variety). There is also a pink variety, but it does not exhibit this kind of color phenomenon.

Aquamarine

To dream of aquamarine signifies the making of new friends; to wear aquamarine earrings brings love and affection. Aquamarine, a universal symbol of youth, hope, and health, blesses those born in March. (Prior to the fifteenth century it was thought to be the birthstone for those born in October.)

Aquamarine is a member of the important beryl family, which includes emerald, but aquamarine is less brittle and more durable than emerald. Aquamarine ranges in color from light blue to bluish green to deep blue, which is the most valuable and desirable color. Do not purchase a shallow-cut stone, since the color will become paler as dirt accumulates on the back. It is a very wearable gem, clear and brilliant, and, unlike emerald, is available with excellent clarity even in very large sizes, although these are becoming scarce today. Aquamarines are still widely available in sizes up to 15 carats, but 10-carat sizes with fine color and clarity are becoming scarce and are more expensive. Long considered a beautiful and moderately priced gem, it is now entering the "expensive" classification for stones in larger sizes with a good deep blue color.

One must be careful not to mistake blue topaz for aquamarine. While topaz is an equally beautiful gem, it is usually much less expensive since it is usually treated to obtain its desirable color. For those who can't afford an aquamarine, however, blue topaz is an excellent alternative—as long as it is properly represented . . . and priced.

Also, note that many aquamarine-colored synthetic spinels are erroneously sold as aquamarine.

Beryl (Golden Beryl and Morganite)

As early as A.D. 1220 the virtues of beryl were well known to man. Beryl provided help against foes in battle or litigation, made the wearer unconquerable, but at the same time friendly and likable, and also sharpened his intellect and cured him of laziness. Today beryl is still considered important, but primarily for aesthetic reasons. The variety of colors in which it is found, its wonderful clarity (except for emerald), its brilliance, and its durability (again with the exception of emerald) have given the various varieties of beryl tremendous appeal.

Most people are familiar with the blue variety, aquamarine, and the green variety, emerald. Few as yet know the pink or orange variety, morganite, and the beautiful yellow to yellow green variety, referred to as golden beryl. (Some orange varieties are heated to produce the more popular pink color and then sold as morganite.) These gems have only recently found their place in the jewelry world but are already being shown in fabulous pieces made by the greatest designers. While not inexpensive, they still offer excellent value and beauty.

Beryl has also been found in many other colors—lilac, salmon, orange, red, sea green, as well as colorless. While most of these varieties are not as yet available to any but the most ardent rock hound, the orange varieties are fairly common and can still be found for under $125 per carat.

Bloodstone (Heliotrope)

Believed by the ancient Greeks to have fallen from heaven, this stone has held a prominent place throughout history, and even into modern times, as a great curative. It was (and still is in some parts of the world) believed capable of stopping every type of bleeding, clearing bloodshot eyes, acting as an antidote for snakebite, and relieving urinary troubles. Today there are people who wear bloodstone amulets to prevent sunstroke and headache, and to provide protection against the evil eye.

The birthstone for March, bloodstone is a more or less opaque, dark green variety of quartz with specks of red jasper (a variety of quartz) spattering red throughout the dark green field. It is particularly popular for men's rings (perhaps they need more protection from illness?). It is most desirable when the green isn't so dark as to approach black and the red flecks are roundish and pronounced. It has fair durability and is fairly readily available and inexpensive.

Chrysoberyl and Cat's-Eye

The chrysoberyl family is very interesting because all three of its varieties—alexandrite (already discussed), cat's-eye, and chrysoberyl—while chemically alike, are quite distinct from one another in their optical characteristics and bear no visible resemblance to one another.

Chrysoberyl in its cat's-eye variety has long been used as a charm to guard against evil spirits, and one can understand why, given the pronounced eye effect (the eye could see all, and it watched out for its wearer). But it was also believed that to dream of cat's-eye signified treachery. On still another hand, it symbolized "long life"—perhaps as a result of being protected from the evil eye.

Cat's-eye is a translucent gem ranging in color from a honey yellow or honey brown to yellowish green to an almost emerald green. It has a velvety or silklike texture, and when properly cut displays a brilliant whitish line of light right down the center, appearing almost to be lighted from inside. (Don't confuse this with the common quartz variety of cat's-eye, which is often brown and called tigereye; it has a much weaker eye and weaker color altogether.) This phenomenon is produced only in cabochons (cabs). It is very hard.

To see the effect properly, the stone should be viewed under a single light source, coming if possible from directly overhead. If the line is not exactly in the center, its value is reduced. The line does move from side to side when the stone is moved about—probably another reason ancient people believed it capable of seeing all and guarding its wearer.

The stone called chrysoberyl, on the other hand, is a brilliant, transparent, very clear, and very durable stone found in yellow, yellow green, and green varieties. This is another stone that still offers excellent value. It's a real beauty, very moderately priced, and just beginning to be appreciated and to appear on the jewelry scene.

Chrysoprase and Carnelian

Chrysoprase has long been the subject of marvelous stories. In the 1800s, it was believed that a thief sentenced to be hanged or beheaded would immediately escape if he placed a chrysoprase in his mouth. Of course, it might be hard to obtain one unless he just happened to carry one around! And Alexander the Great was believed to have worn a "prase" in his girdle during battle, to ensure victory.

Chrysoprase is an inexpensive, highly translucent, bright, light to dark green variety of quartz. Its color is often very uniform and can be very lovely in jewelry. (But for many years it has been dyed to enhance the color, where necessary.) It is another stone that is usually cut in cabochon style. It has become very popular for jewelry as a fashion accessory. Do not confuse it with jade, however. It is sometimes called "Australian jade" and is sometimes misrepresented as real jade.

If you're the timid sort, carnelian is the stone for you. "The wearing of carnelians is recommended to those who have a weak voice or are timid in speech, for the warm-colored stone will give them the courage they lack so that they will speak both boldly and well," reports G. F. Kunz.

This stone is especially revered by Moslems, because Muhammad himself wore a silver ring set with a carnelian engraved for use as a seal.

Napoleon I, while on a campaign in Egypt, picked up with his own hands (apparently from the battlefield) an unusual octagonal carnelian, upon which was engraved the legend "The Slave Abraham Relying Upon The Merciful [God]." He wore it with him always and bequeathed it to his nephew.

Carnelian, one of the accepted birthstones for August, is a reddish orange variety of quartz. A moderately hard, translucent to opaque stone, its warm uniform color and fair durability have made it a favorite. It is often found in antique jewelry and lends itself to engraving or carving (especially in cameos). It is still a relatively inexpensive stone with great warmth and beauty and offers an excellent choice for jewelry to be worn as an accessory with today's fashion colors.

Coral

Coral, which for twenty centuries or more was classed with precious gems and can be found adorning ancient amulets alongside diamond, ruby, emerald, and pearl, had been "experimentally proved" by the sixteenth century to cure madness, give wisdom, stop the flow of blood from a wound, calm storms, and of course enable the traveler to safely cross broad rivers. It was also known to prevent sterility. This was certainly a powerful gem!

Red coral symbolizes attachment, devotion, and protection against plague and pestilence. And one unique quality . . . it loses its color when a friend of the wearer is about to die! There is one catch, however. To effectively exercise its power, it should not be altered by man's hands but should be worn in its natural, uncut state. This perhaps is why one often sees this stone in necklaces or pins in its natural state.

Coral lost its popularity for a while, but has been steadily gaining in popularity in recent years. It is a semitranslucent to opaque material that, formed from a colony of marine invertebrates, is primarily a skeletal calcium carbonate gem. The formations while seen in the water look like tree branches. Coral occurs in a variety of colors— white, pink, orange, red, and black. One of the most expensive varieties, very popular in recent years and used extensively in fine jewelry, is angel skin coral. This is a whitish variety highlighted with a faint blush of pink or peach. Today the rarest variety, and the most expensive, is blood coral, also called noble or oxblood coral. This is a very deep red variety and shouldn't be confused with the more common orangy red varieties. The best red comes from the seas around Italy; the whites from Japanese waters; the blacks (which we personally don't find very attractive, and which are also different chemically) from Hawaii and Mexico.

Coral is usually cabochon cut, often carved, but is also fairly frequently found in jewelry fashioned "in the rough" (uncut) in certain countries where there is still a belief that coral has magical powers that are lost with cutting. It is a fairly soft stone, so some caution should be exercised when wearing. Also, because of its calcium composition, you must be careful to avoid contact with acid, such as vinegar in a salad that you might toss with your hands.

Also, be a cautious buyer for this gem as well—glass and plastic imitations are commonplace.

Garnet

If you are loyal, devoted, and energetic, perhaps the garnet is your stone. Or if not, perhaps you should obtain some! Red garnets were "known" to promote sincerity, stop hemorrhaging or other loss of blood, cure inflammatory diseases, and cure anger and discord. And if you engrave a well-formed lion image upon it, it will protect and preserve honors and health, cure the wearer of all disease, bring him honors, and guard him from all perils in traveling. All in all, quite a worthwhile stone.

The garnet family is one of the most exciting families in the gem world. A hard, durable, often very brilliant stone, available in many colors (greens, reds, yellows, oranges), it offers far greater versatility and opportunity for the jewelry trade than has yet been capitalized upon. Depending upon the variety, quality, and size, lovely garnets are available for under $20 per carat or more than $3,000 per carat. Garnet is also mistaken for other (usually more expensive) gems— green garnet, tsavorite, is one of the most beautiful, and all but a few would assume it was an emerald of the finest quality. In fact, it is "clearer," more brilliant, and more durable. There is also a rarer green garnet, called demantoid, which costs slightly more than tsavorite but which, although slightly softer, has more fire. These gems offer fine alternatives to the person desiring a lovely green gem who can't afford emerald. While still rare, expensive gems themselves, they are far less expensive than an emerald of comparable quality. Garnet also occurs in certain shades of red that have been taken for some varieties of ruby. And in yellow it has been confused with precious topaz.

Garnet can be found in almost every color and shade except blue. It is best known in a deep red variety, sometimes with a brownish cast, but it is commonly found in orangish brown shades, and brilliant wine red shades as well. Other colors include orange, red purple, violet, and pink. A nontransparent variety, grossularite, has a jadelike appearance and may be mistaken for jade when cut into cabochons or carved.

There is also a star garnet found in the United States that is a reddish to purple variety which displays a faint four-rayed or six-rayed star, similar to the six-rayed star ruby but not as pronounced.

Hematite and Marcasite

Hematite is a must for the lawyer, for it ensures for its wearer "alertness, vivacity, and success in litigation." It is also believed to ensure sexual impulse, so if you know of someone with a problem, this may make a "thoughtful" gift.

Hematite is an iron oxide (like iron rust), a metallic, opaque stone found in iron-mining areas. It takes a very brilliant, metallic polish that can look almost like silver, or almost pure black (or gunmetal blue). It was and is popular for use in carving hollow cameo portraits known as intaglio.

Marcasite, the tiny, glittering stone with a brassy-colored luster often seen in old belt buckles and costume jewelry, is a relative of hematite. But *most* "marcasite" seen in jewelry is *not* marcasite, but pyrite (fool's gold)—another brassy-colored metallic mineral.

Iolite

This is a transparent, usually very clean, blue gem, ranging from deep blue to light gray blue to yellowish grey. It is sometimes called dichroite and in its sapphire blue color is sometimes referred to as water sapphire or lynx sapphire. It is a lovely, brilliant stone but not as durable as sapphire. We are just beginning to see this stone in jewelry, and it is still a good value. It is abundant, still very low priced, and one of the most attractive jewelry options for the near future.

Jade

Jade has long been revered by the Chinese. White jade (yes, white) was believed by the early Chinese to quiet intestinal disturbances and black jade to give strength and power. A very early written Chinese symbol for king was a string of jade beads, and jade beads are still used in China as a symbol of high rank and authority. Jade is also an important part of the Chinese wedding ceremony (the "jade ceremony" holds a prominent place here), for jade is considered the "concentrated essence of love."

Jade is a very tough, although not too hard, translucent to opaque gem, often seen in jewelry and carvings. There are really two types of jade—jadeite and nephrite—which are really two separate and distinct minerals differing from one another in weight, hardness, and color range.

Jadeite is the most expensive, more desirable variety. It was the most sought after by the Chinese after 1740. It is *not* found in China, however, but in Burma. Some fine jadeite also comes from Guatemala. It comes in a much wider range of colors than nephrite: green, mottled green and white, whitish gray, pink, brown, mauve, yellow, orange, and lilac. In fact, it comes in almost every color. But with the exception of green (which comes in shades that vary from pale to a beautiful emerald green), colored jade is usually pale and unevenly colored. The most desirable color is a rich emerald green sometimes referred to as imperial jade. Smooth, evenly colored pieces of this jadeite are highly prized. In fact, they can be classed as precious stones today. The mottled pieces of irregular green, often seen carved, are less valuable, but still more rare and valuable than nephrite jade.

Nephrite jade, the old and true Chinese jade, resembles jadeite but is slightly softer (yet slightly tougher and thus less easily broken) and has a much more limited range of color. It is regularly seen in dark green shades (sometimes so dark as to look black: black jade), usually fashioned in cabochon cut, or round beads, or in carvings. Nephrite green is a more sober green than the apple green or emerald green color of good jadeite. It is closer in color to a dark, sage green or spinach green. Nephrite may also be a creamier color, as in mutton fat jade. Any fine Chinese carving that is more than 230 years old is carved from nephrite (jadeite was unknown to the Chinese before 1740).

Nephrite has been found in many countries, including the United States, where in the late nineteenth century Chinese miners panning for gold in California discovered large boulders of nephrite jade that they sent back to China to be cut or carved. It is also common in Wyoming, Alaska, and British Columbia.

Nephrite jade is much more common than jadeite and is therefore much less expensive. But it is a lovely, popular stone, used extensively in jewelry and carvings.

One must be careful, however, in purchasing jade. You will often see "imperial" jade that is nothing more than a cheap jade that has been dyed. Much of it is treated (usually this means dyed) to enhance its value. The dyeing, however, may be *very* temporary. Black jade is either dyed or very dark green nephrite that looks black. There are also numerous minerals that look like jade and are sold as jade under misleading names, such as "Virginia jade" (a blue green mineral called amazonite, common in Virginia); "Mexican jade" (jade colored or dyed onyx marble); "Potomac jade" (diopside, a green mineral). "Pennsylvania jade," "Korean jade," "new jade" are all serpentine, similar in appearance to some varieties of jade. Much of the intricately and beautifully carved jade is actually serpentine, which can be scratched easily with a knife.

Soapstone may also look like jade to the amateur, especially when beautifully carved. This stone is so soft that it can easily be scratched with a pin, hairpin, or point of a pen. (But don't scratch it in a noticeable place.) It is very much less expensive than comparable varieties of jade, and it is softer and less durable.

Jade is a wonderful stone. Imperial jade is breathtaking. It is no wonder it was the emperor's stone. But jade has long been "copied"—misrepresented and altered. Just be sure you know you are buying what you think you are buying. And then enjoy it!

Labradorite

Labradorite is a fascinating stone, starting to appear in some of the more distinctive jewelry salons. A member of the feldspar family, it is a grayish, almost opaque stone, within which one will observe startlingly brilliant flashes of peacock blue, greens, and/or yellows at certain angles. It is usually cut in cabochon style. There are some glass imitations, but they don't come close to the real thing. This is a stone that is still relatively inexpensive and one to consider seriously if you want something striking and unusual.

Lapis Lazuli

Lapis, a birthstone for December, has been highly prized since ancient Babylonian and Egyptian times. An amulet of "great power" was formed when lapis was worked into the form of an eye and ornamented with gold; in fact, so powerful that sometimes these eyes were put to rest on the limbs of a mummy. In addition, it was recognized as a symbol for capacity, ability, success, and divine favor.

Genuine lapis is a natural blue opaque stone of intense, brilliant, deep blue color. It sometimes possesses small, sparkling gold- or silver-colored flecks (pyrite inclusions), although the finest quality is a deep, even blue with a purplish tint or undertone and no trace of these flecks. Occasionally it may be blue mottled with white.

Don't confuse genuine lapis with the cheaper "Swiss lapis" or "Italian lapis," which aren't lapis at all. These are natural stones (usually quartz) artificially colored to look like lapis lazuli. Genuine lapis is often represented as "Russian lapis," although it doesn't always come from Russia. The finest lapis comes from Afghanistan.

Lapis has become very fashionable, and the finest-quality lapis is becoming more rare and more expensive. This has resulted in an abundance of lapis that has been "color-improved." It is often fashioned today with other gems—pearls, crystal, coral—that make particularly striking fashion accessories.

Sodalite is sometimes confused with the more expensive, and rarer, lapis and used as a substitute for it. However, sodalite rarely contains the silvery or golden flecks typical of most lapis. It may have some white veining, but more commonly it just exhibits the fine lapis blue without any markings. The lapis substitutes do transmit some light through the edges of the stone; lapis does not, since it is opaque.

Dyed chalcedony (quartz), glass, and plastic imitations are common. One quick and easy test to identify genuine lapis is to put a drop of hydrochloric acid on the lapis which will immediately produce the odor of a rotten egg. (This test should be administered only by a professional, however, since hydrochloric acid can be dangerous.)

Malachite and Azurite

Malachite must have been the answer to a mother's prayer. Attached to the neck of a child, it would ease its pain when cutting teeth. Also, tied over a woman in labor, it would ensure an easier, faster birth; and it could also cure diseases of the eye. More important, however, it was believed capable of protecting from the evil eye and bringing good luck.

Malachite is also popular today, but perhaps more because of its exquisite color and a softness that makes it very popular for carving. Malachite is a copper ore that comes in a brilliant kelly green, marked with bands or concentric striping in contrasting shades of the same basic green. It is opaque and takes a good polish, but it is soft and should not be worn in rings. This softness, however, makes it a favorite substance for use in carved bases, boxes, beads, statues, spheres, etc. It is also used in pins, pendants, and necklaces (usually of malachite beads).

Azurite is also a copper ore, but it occurs in a very vivid deep blue, similarly marked. Occasionally one will come across both colors intermingled in brilliant combinations of color and striking patterns. Both make beautiful jewelry and lovely carvings.

Caution: Never clean malachite or azurite with any product containing ammonia. In seconds the ammonia will remove all of the polish, which will significantly reduce its beauty.

Moonstone (Feldspar)

Moonstone is definitely a good luck stone, especially for lovers. As a gift for lovers the moonstone holds a high rank, for it is believed to arouse one's tender passion and to give lovers the ability to foretell their future—good or ill. (But to get this information, the stone must be placed in the mouth while the moon is full.) Perhaps a more important use, however, was in amulets made of moonstone, which would protect men from epilepsy and guarantee a greater fruit-crop yield when hung on fruit trees (it assisted all vegetation).

The name "moonstone" is probably derived from the theory that one can observe the lunar month through the stone—that a small white spot appears in the stone as the new moon begins and gradually moves toward the stone's center, getting always larger, until at full moon the spot has taken the shape of a full moon in the center of the stone.

Moonstone is a member of the feldspar family. It is a transparent, milky-white variety in which can be seen a floating opalescent white or blue light within the stone's body. It is a popular stone for rings because as the hand moves the effect of the brilliant light/color is more pronounced. The bluer color is the finer and more desirable, but it is becoming rare in today's market, particularly in large sizes.

There are some glass imitations of moonstone, but compared to the real thing they are not very good.

Obsidian

Obsidian was widely used by the Mexicans, probably because of its brilliant polished surface, for making images of their god Tezcatlipoca, and mirrors to divine the future. It has also been found in Egypt, fashioned into masks.

Obsidian is a smoky brown to black (and sometimes a mixture of both), semitranslucent to opaque glass. But it is *natural* glass, not man-made. It is formed by volcanic activity and is also called volcanic glass. One variety, snow-flake obsidian, exhibits white spots resembling snowflakes against or mingled with the black; some obsidian exhibits a strong iridescence; and some obsidian exhibits a sheen from within, as seen in moonstone.

Jewelry made from obsidian, which is available in great quantity and is very inexpensive, is a popular fashion accessory. It is particularly popular in Mexican and Indian jewelry, and is seen fairly extensively in the West and in Mexico. One must exercise some caution, however, because it is glass and can be scratched or cracked easily.

Onyx

Onyx is not a good-omen stone, and it is certainly not one I would recommend for young lovers. It is believed to bear an evil omen for lovers, to provoke discord and separate them. Worn around the neck, it was said to cool the ardors of love. (The close union and yet strong contrast between the layers of black and white in some varieties may have suggested this.) It was also believed to cause discord in general, create disharmony among friends, bring bad dreams and broken sleep to its wearer, and cause pregnant women to give birth prematurely.

But there isn't complete agreement as to its unlucky nature. Indians and Persians believe that wearing onyx will protect them from the evil eye, and that when placed on the stomach of a woman in labor it would reduce the labor pain and bring on earlier delivery. So you choose—good or bad?

Onyx is a lovely banded, semitranslucent to opaque quartz. It comes naturally in a variety of colors—reds, oranges, reddish orange, apricot, and shades of brown from cream to dark, often alternating with striking bands of white. The banding in onyx is *straight*, while *curved* bands occur in the variety of quartz known as agate. Onyx is used extensively for cameo and other carving work. It is also frequently dyed.

Let's discuss black onyx for a moment. Black onyx isn't onyx and doesn't occur black in nature. It is chalcedony (another variety of quartz) dyed black. It is *always* dyed, and may be banded or solid black.

Do not confuse the quartz variety onyx discussed above with cave onyx, which is found in the stalactites and stalagmites of underground caves. Cave onyx is a different material altogether. It is much softer, lacks the color variety, and is much less expensive than quartz onyx.

Opal

The opal has suffered from an unfortunate reputation as being an evil stone and bearing an ill omen. There are several explanations for the ominous superstitions surrounding this wonderful gem, but I'd rather take this time to mention some of its good association and leave you with an assurance that the evil association has never been merited and probably resulted from a careless reading of Sir Walter Scott's *Anne of Geierstein.*

Among the ancients opal was a symbol of fidelity and assurance, and in later history it became strongly associated with religious emotion and prayer. It was believed to have a strong therapeutic value for diseases of the eye, and worn as an amulet it would make the wearer immune from all such disease as well as increase the powers of the eyes and the mind. Further, many believed that to the extent the colors of red and green were seen, the therapeutic powers of stones of those colors (ruby and emerald) were also to be enjoyed by the wearer—the power to stop bleeding, etc. (ruby); the power to cure kidney diseases, etc. (emerald). The black opal was particularly highly prized as the luck stone of anyone lucky enough to own one!

This stone, whose brilliance and vibrant colors resemble the colors of the fall, is certainly appropriate as a birthstone for October. When we try to describe the opal, we realize how insufficient the English language is. It is unique among the gems, displaying an array of very brilliant miniature rainbow effects, all mixed up together.

Its most outstanding characteristic is this unusual, intense display of many colors flashing out like mini-rainbows. This effect is created by opal's formation process, which is very different from that of other gems. Opal is composed of hydrated silica spheres. The mini-rainbows seen in most opals result from light interference created by these spheres. The arrangement of the spheres, which vary in size and pattern, is responsible for the different colors seen.

Opal is usually cut flat or in cabochon, since there is no additional brilliance to be captured by a good faceting job. Color is everything. The more brilliant the color, the more valuable the gem. It is probably truer of opal than any other stone that the more beautiful the stone and its color, the more it will cost.

The finest of all is the black opal. Black opals are usually a deep gray or grayish black with flashes of incredibly brilliant color dancing around within and about the stone as it is turned. One must be careful when purchasing a black opal, however, to ensure that it is not a doublet or triplet, a stone composed of two or three pieces of stone glued together. There are many such doublets on the market because of the black opal's rarity, beauty, and extremely high cost (one the size of a lima bean could cost $50,000 today). The black opal doublet provides an affordable option to one who loves them but can't afford them. But it also provides another opportunity for misrepresentation that can be very costly to the consumer.

Generally speaking, purity of color, absence of dead spots (called *trueness*), flawlessness, and intensity or brilliance of color are the primary variables affecting value. Those with an abundance of red are usually the most expensive; those strong in blue and green are equally beautiful but not as rare, so their price is somewhat less. Some opals are very transparent and are classified as "jelly," "semijelly," or "water" opals.

While there are imitations and synthetics, for the most part they are still not worth mentioning. The synthetic opal, however, is being used extensively. Also, the color of black opals can be improved by treatment, and treated opals are encountered frequently. So let us reiterate—make *sure* you know what you are getting. And as we've mentioned many times, before buying shop around. This holds truer for opal, perhaps, than any other stone.

One word of caution must also be offered: Opals require special care because some tend to dry and crack. Avoid exposure to anything that is potentially drying. And, believe it or not, bathing the opal occasionally in olive oil, or coating it with olive oil when not in use, will help preserve it (but *not* soaking it—soaking some opals for only a few hours can cause them to lose some or nearly all of their fire.)

Peridot

Today's birthstone for August, peridot was also a favorite of the ancients. This lovely transparent yellowish green to deep chartreuse stone was quite a powerful gem. It was considered an aid to friendship and was also believed to free the mind of envious thoughts. (Which is probably why it was an aid to friendship.) Because of its yellowish green color, it was also believed to cure or prevent diseases of the liver and dropsy. And, if that's not enough, if worn on the left arm it would protect the wearer from the evil eye.

It is also popular today, but probably more for its depth of green color than its professed powers. While not particularly brilliant, the richness of its color is exceptional. It comes in shades of yellowish green to darker, purer green colors. It is still widely available in small sizes but larger sizes are becoming scarce, so prices in larger sizes are now fairly high for good quality material.

Some caution should also be exercised in wearing peridot. It is not a very hard stone and may scratch easily. Also, some stones may look like peridot (green sapphire, green tourmaline) and be mistaken for peridot and be misrepresented.

Quartz

Quartz is the most versatile of any of the gem families. It includes among its members more variety and a larger number of gems than any other three mineral families together. As someone once said, "If in doubt, say quartz."

The quartz minerals, for the most part, are relatively inexpensive gems that offer a wide range of pleasing color alternatives both in transparent and nontransparent varieties (from translucent to opaque). They are reasonably hard stones, and while not very brilliant in the transparent varieties, still create lovely, affordable jewelry.

Some of these gems have been discussed in separate sections, but we will provide a list here with brief descriptions of most of the quartz family members.

Transparent Varieties

Amethyst (see page 147). Lilac to purple.

Citrine (often called quartz topaz, citrine topaz, or topaz, all of which are misleading. The correct name for this stone is citrine). It is yellow, amber, to amber brown. This is the most commonly seen "topaz" in today's marketplace and is, unfortunately, too often confused with precious topaz because of the careless use of the name topaz. While a pleasing stone in terms of color, and fairly durable, citrine is slightly softer and has less brilliance than precious topaz. It also lacks the subtle color shading, the pinkier yellow or pinkish amber shades, which lend to precious topaz a distinctive color difference. (Much citrine is made by heat-treating purple amethyst.)

Citrine is also much less expensive than precious topaz. It should never be represented as topaz, which technically is "precious" or "imperial" topaz. Unfortunately, it often is. For example, "topaz" birthstone jewelry is almost always citrine (or a worthless synthetic). So ask, "Is this citrine or precious topaz?" (And get the answer in writing if you are told, "Precious topaz.")

Citrine is plentiful in all sizes, and can be made into striking jewelry, especially in very large sizes, for a relatively small investment (while precious topaz of fine quality is scarce in sizes over 7 carats, and *very* expensive).

Praseolite. A pale green transparent variety produced by heating amethyst.

Rock crystal. Water clear. Used in old jewelry for rondelles (a type of small bead resembling a doughnut). Cut (faceted) crystal beads were also common in older jewelry. Today, however, *crystal* usually refers to glass.

Rose quartz. Light to deep pink. This stone has been very popular for many years for use in carved pieces—beads, statues, ashtrays, fine lamp bases, and pins and brooches. Rarely clear, this stone is usually seen in cabochon cut, rounded beads, or carvings rather than in faceted styles. Once very inexpensive, it is becoming more costly, particularly in the finer deep pink shades. But the color of rose quartz is especially pleasing and it offers an excellent choice for use in fashion accessory jewelry.

One must be somewhat cautious with rose quartz, however, because it tends to crack more easily than most other varieties of quartz if struck or exposed to a blow (due to the inclusions or internal fractures that are also responsible for the absence of clarity in this stone).

Smoky quartz. A pale to rich smoky brown variety, sometimes mistaken for or misrepresented as smoky topaz or topaz. Also very plentiful and becoming popular for use in very large sizes for beautiful brooches, large dinner rings, etc.

Translucent to Opaque Varieties

Agate and chalcedony. All colors and varieties of markings are seen in this wonderful ornamental gem. Among them you'll find, to mention a few: banded agate; moss agate, a fascinating white or milky agate that looks as though it actually has black, brown, or green moss growing within; eye agate, which has an eyeball effect; plume agate, which looks like it's filled with beautiful feather plumes. The colors and "scenes" in agate are infinite. While agate is usually an inexpensive stone, some varieties or special stones with very unusual scenes or markings can be quite expensive.

Carnelian, sard, and sardonyx are reddish, orange, apricot, and brown varieties of chalcedony and are often seen in cameo or other carving work. Black onyx is a dyed chalcedony; chrysoprase is green chalcedony, often dyed green.

The unusual colors and markings of agate made it very highly regarded by the ancients and revered throughout history, even to the present day. It was believed to make wearers "agreeable and persuasive and give them God's favor." Other virtues claimed for agate wearers include giving to the wearer victory and strength and also protection from tempests and lightning, guarding its wearer from all dangers, enabling him to overcome all terrestrial obstacles, and imparting to him a bold heart.

Wearing agate ornaments could also cure insomnia and ensure good dreams. In the middle of the 1800s (and continuing to the present in some parts of the world) amulets made from eye agate (brown or black agate with a white ring in the center) were so popular that agate cutters in Germany had time for cutting little else. The "eye" was believed to take on the watchfulness of one's guardian spirit and protect the wearer from the evil eye by neutralizing its power. At one time these amulets commanded an incredible price.

Whatever their real power, they are fascinating stones, some quite mesmerizing in their unusual beauty. They are often seen in antique jewelry as well as contemporary pieces. One must be careful, however, to exercise some caution in wear to protect from knocks, as some varieties are more fragile than others. Also, agate is frequently dyed, so it is important to ask whether the color is natural, and to be sure that it is not another less valuable stone, dyed to look like a special variety of agate.

Aventurine. A lovely pale to medium green semitranslucent stone with tiny sparkling flecks of mica within. This stone makes very lovely cabochon or bead jewelry at a very affordable price. It is occasionally misrepresented as jade, but the mica flecks provide an immediate indicator that it is aventurine quartz instead (although sometimes the flecks are so small that they cannot be seen easily). Be aware, however, that there are some glass imitations which are fairly good.

Bloodstone (see page 149). Dark green with red spots.

Cat's-Eye. A pale yellowish green stone that when cut in cabochon style produces a streak of light down the center that creates an eye effect. (This phenomenon is due to the presence of fiberlike inclusions.) Its center line is weaker, its color paler, and its cost much less than true cat's-eye from the chrysoberyl family. But it is nonetheless an attractive stone that makes attractive, affordable jewelry.

Chrysocolla. The true chrysocolla is a very soft copper mineral, too soft for jewelry use. However, quartz that has been naturally impregnated or stained with chrysocolla has good hardness and the same brilliant blue green, highly translucent color. We will probably see more quartz chrysocolla in jewelry in coming years.

Chrysoprase (see page 150). Bright light to dark green, highly translucent stone, and often of very even color. Sometimes misrepresented or confused for jade.

Jasper. Opaque red, yellow, brown (or sometimes gray), and green. Usually strongly marked in terms of the contrast between the green and other colors in an almost blotchlike or veinlike pattern. The red and green combination is the most popular, although there are more than fifty types of jasper of various colors and patterns.

Jasper was believed in ancient cultures to bring rain and also to protect its wearer from the bites of poisonous creatures. It was believed to have as diverse a power as the colors and veins in which it came, so there were many uses and magical powers associated with jasper.

Jasper offers interesting color contrast and variety, and is being used increasingly in today's fashion accessory jewelry.

Petrified wood. Sections of trees or limbs that have been replaced by quartz-type silica and transformed into a mineral after centuries of immersion in silica-rich water under extreme pressure. Usually red, reddish brown, or brown. Not often seen in jewelry.

Tigereye. A golden, yellowish, reddish, and sometimes bluish variety of quartz that produces a bright shimmering line (or lines) of light, which when cut in a cabochon will produce an eye. The eye will move when the stone is turned from side to side. It is inexpensive, but very popular for fashion accessory jewelry and men's cuff links and rings.

Rhodochrosite

Rhodochrosite is a newcomer to the jewelry business. While sought by rock hounds for many years and a favorite of beginning lapidaries, rhodochrosite appeared only occasionally outside of rock and mineral shows, frequented by hobbyists.

A member of the carbonate mineral group, rhodochrosite is a relatively soft stone occurring in both transparent (rare) and non-transparent varieties. For practical purposes, we will discuss the non-transparent variety, which is the more common.

It is a lovely red to almost white color, often with agatelike curved lines creating a design in contrasting shades of red or pink. It may occasionally occur in an orangy tone, but this is poorer-quality material. The finest color is a medium to deep rose, preferably with the curved banding. It has long been popular for certain ornamental objects (spheres, boxes, eggs) but only recently for jewelry. Today, bead necklaces using rhodochrosite beads alternating with other stones, or gold beads, are becoming particularly popular. We will see more rhodochrosite on the market in coming years. It is soft, however, and some caution should be used in wearing to avoid unnecessary abuse.

Scapolite

We will dwell very briefly on this stone, since it may soon make a debut on the jewelry scene.

Rediscovered in Brazil after a forty-year hiatus and also recently discovered in Kenya, scapolite is a nice, transparent, fairly durable stone occurring in a range of colors from colorless to yellow, light red, orange to greenish to bluish gray, violet, and violet blue. The orange, light red, and whitish stones may also occur as semitransparent stones, which may show a cat's-eye effect (chatoyancy) when cut into cabochons.

The most likely to appear in jewelry are the violets and yellows, and possibly orange cat's-eyes. They might easily be mistaken for yellow beryl or certain quartz minerals (amethyst, citrine).

The bottom line here is that we will have to wait and see. Availability will determine use and cost.

Serpentine

Serpentine derives its name from its similarity to the green, speckled skin of the serpent. Amulets of serpentine were worn for protection from serpent bites, stings of poisonous reptiles, and poison in general. A king was reputed to have insisted that his chalice be made of serpentine, as it was believed that if a poisoned drink were put into a serpentine vessel, the vessel would sweat on the outside. The effectiveness of medicine was increased when drunk from a serpentine vessel.

Serpentine is often used as a jade substitute. It is a translucent to semitranslucent stone occurring in light to dark yellowish green to greenish yellow. One variety is used for decorative wall facings and table and counter surfaces, but some of the more attractive green varieties so closely resemble jadeite or nephrite jade that they are used in carvings and jewelry, and are often misrepresented as jade. Common serpentine is also sometimes dyed a jadelike color. One lovely green variety, williamsite, which is a very pleasing deep green, often with small black flecks within, is often sold as "Pennsylvania jade." It is pretty, but it is *not* jade. Another variety of serpentine, bowenite, is also sold today as "Korean jade" or "new jade." Again, it is pretty but is *not* jade.

Serpentine is softer than jade, less durable, and much more common, which its price should reflect.

It is a lovely stone in its own right, and makes a nice alternative to jade. While it has been around for a long time (too often, however, represented as jade), we are just beginning to see this stone used frequently in necklaces and other fine jewelry under its own name.

Sodalite

This stone has already been discussed under lapis. It is a dark blue semitransparent to semitranslucent stone used frequently as a substitute for the rarer, more expensive lapis. While it may have some white veining, it does not have the golden or silver flecks that are characteristic of lapis. If you do not see these shiny flecks, suspect that it is probably sodalite.

Spinel

Spinel is one of the loveliest of the gems but hasn't yet been given due credit and respect. It is usually compared to sapphire or ruby, rather than being recognized for its own intrinsic beauty and value. There is also a common belief that spinel (and similarly zircon) is synthetic rather than natural, when in fact it is one of nature's most beautiful products (although synthetic spinel is also seen frequently on the market).

Spinel commonly occurs in red orange (flame spinel), light to dark orangy red, light to dark slightly grayish blue, greenish blue, grayish green, and dark to light purple to violet. It also occurs in yellow and in an opaque variety—black. When compared to the blue of sapphire or the red of ruby, its color is considered less intense, but its brilliance can be greater. If you appreciate these spinel colors for themselves, they are quite pleasing. The most popular are red (more orange than the ruby red) and blue (a strong Bromo-Seltzer-bottle blue).

Spinel may be confused with or misrepresented as one of many stones—ruby, sapphire, zircon, amethyst, garnet, synthetic ruby/ sapphire or synthetic spinel—as well as glass. The synthetic is often used to make composite stones such as doublets. Spinel is a fairly hard, fairly durable stone, possessing a nice brilliance, and still a good value.

This stone is becoming more and more popular today, and may, therefore, become more expensive if current trends continue.

Spodumene (Kunzite and Hiddenite)

Spodumene is another gem relatively new to widespread jewelry use. The most popular varieties are kunzite and hiddenite.

Kunzite is a very lovely brilliant stone occurring in delicate lilac, pink, or violet shades. Its color can fade in strong light, and so it has become known as an "evening" stone. Also, while hard, it can break easily if it receives a sharp blow from certain directions. It is not recommended for rings for this reason unless set in a protective mounting. But it is a lovely gem, whose low cost makes it attractive in large sizes, and an excellent choice for lovely, dramatic jewelry design.

Hiddenite is rarer. Light green or yellow green varieties are available, but the emerald green varieties are scarce. As with kunzite, it is hard but brittle, so care must be exercised in wear.

Spodumene also occurs in many other shades of color, all pale but very clear and brilliant. Only blue is currently missing (but who knows what may yet be discovered in Africa?).

Spodumene is still fairly inexpensive and is an excellent choice for contemporary jewelry design. Be careful, however, as it can be confused with topaz, tourmaline, spinel, or beryl. Also, synthetic corundum or spinel, doublets, and glass can be mistaken for this gem.

Titanite (Sphene)

This is another "new" gem that offers great promise. While it has been highly regarded for many years, its relative scarcity prevented its widescale use in jewelry. Today, however, new sources have been discovered and we are beginning to see greater availability.

This is a beautiful, brilliant stone, with a diamondlike (adamantine) luster and fire that is even greater than in diamond. Unfortunately, it is soft. Its colors range from grass green to golden yellow to brown.

There is need for some caution because of this stone's softness. We suggest that it is especially suitable for pendants, earrings, brooches, and protective ring settings.

Topaz

True topaz, symbol of love and affection, aid to sweetness of disposition, and birthstone for November, is one of nature's most wonderful and least-known families.

The true topaz is rarely seen in jewelry stores. Unfortunately, most people know only the quartz (citrine) topaz, or glass. In the past almost any yellow stone was called topaz. True topaz is very beautiful and versatile.

Topaz occurs not only in the transparent yellow, yellow brown, orangy brown, and pinky brown colors most popularly associated with it, but also in a very light to medium red (now found naturally in fair supply, although many are produced through heat treatment), very light to light blue (also often the result of treatment, although it does occur naturally on a fairly wide scale), very light green, light greenish yellow, violet, and colorless.

Topaz is a hard, brilliant stone with a fine color range, but it is much rarer and much more expensive than the stones commonly sold as topaz. It is also heavier than its imitators.

There are many misleading names to suggest that a stone is topaz when it is not, for example, "Rio topaz," "Madeira topaz," "Spanish topaz," and "Palmeira topaz." They are types of citrine (quartz) and should be represented as such.

Blue topaz has become very popular in recent years; most of it treated (there is no way yet to determine which have been treated and which are natural). It closely resembles the finest aquamarine (which is very expensive today) and offers a very attractive, and much more affordable, alternative to it. Some of the fine, deeper blue treated to-pazes have been found to be radioactive and, according to the Nuclear Regulatory Commission, may be injurious to the wearer.

The true topaz family offers a variety of color options in lovely, clear, brilliant, and durable stones. This family should become more important in the years ahead.

Tourmaline

Tourmaline is a gem of modern times, but nonetheless has found its way to the list of birthstones, becoming an "alternate birthstone" for October. Perhaps this honor results from tourmaline's versatility and broad color range. Or perhaps to the fact that red-and-green tourmaline, in which the red and green occur side by side in the same stone, is reminiscent of the turning of October leaves.

Whatever the case, tourmaline is one of the most versatile of the gem families. It is available in every color, in every tone, from deep to pastel and even with two or more colors appearing in the same stone, side by side. There are bicolored tourmalines (half red and the other half green, for example) and tricolored (one-third blue, one-third green, and one-third yet another color). The fascinating "watermelon" tourmaline looks just like the inside of a watermelon—red in the center surrounded by a green "rind." Tourmaline can also be found in a cat's-eye type.

It is indeed surprising that most people know of tourmaline simply as a common "green" stone. Only today are we beginning to see other lovely varieties of this fascinating gem used in jewelry on any scale:

- Chrome—A particular rare green hue
- Dravite—Yellow to brown
- Indicolite—deep indigo blue, usually with a green undertone
- Rubellite—deep pink to red (as in ruby)
- Siberite—purple
- Verdelite—green varieties

While tourmaline is still a very affordable gem, even in large sizes, the chrome, indicolite, and rubellite varieties are priced (depending on size and quality) anywhere from $300 to $1,000 per carat whole-sale. So much for the "common and inexpensive" myth!

Tourmaline is a fairly hard, durable, brilliant, and very wearable stone with a wide choice of colors. It is also still available in large sizes. It is a stone that without question will play a more and more important role in jewelry in the years ahead.

Turquoise

A birthstone for December, and ranking highest among all the opaque stones, turquoise—the "Turkish stone"—is highly prized throughout Asia and Africa, not only for its particular hue of blue (a beautiful robin's-egg or sky blue) but more important for its prophylactic and therapeutic qualities. The Arabs consider it a lucky stone and have great confidence in its benevolent action. Used in rings, earrings, necklaces, head ornaments, and amulets, it protects the wearer from poison, reptile bites, eye diseases, and the evil eye. It was also believed capable of warning of impending death by changing color. Also, the drinking of water in which turquoise has been dipped or washed was believed to cure bladder ailments. Buddhists revere the turquoise because it is associated with a legend in which a turquoise enabled Buddha to destroy a monster. Even today it is considered a symbol of courage, success, and love. It has also long been associated with American Indian jewelry and art.

Turquoise is an opaque, light to dark blue or blue green stone. The finest color is an intense blue, with poorer qualities tending toward yellowish green. The famous Persian turquoise, which can be a very intense and pleasing blue, is considered a very rare and valuable gem.

All turquoises are susceptible to aging and may turn greenish or possibly darker with age. Also, care must be taken when wearing, both to avoid contact with soap, grease, or other materials that might discolor it, and to protect it from abuse, since turquoise scratches fairly easily.

But exercise caution when buying turquoise. This is a frequently simulated gem. Very fine glass imitations are produced that are difficult to distinguish from the genuine. Very fine adulterated stones, and reconstructed stones (from turquoise powder bonded in plastic) saturate the marketplace, as does synthetic turquoise. There are techniques to quickly distinguish these simulations, so, if in doubt, check it out (and get a complete description on the bill of sale: "genuine, natural turquoise").

Zircon

Known to the ancients as "hyacinth," this gem had many powers, especially for men. While it was known to assist women in childbirth, for men it kept evil spirits and bad dreams away, gave protection against "fascination" and lightning, strengthened their bodies, fortified their hearts, restored appetite, suppressed fat, produced sleep, and banished grief and sadness from the mind.

Zircons are very brilliant transparent stones available in several lovely colors. Unfortunately, zircon suffers from a strange misconception that it is a synthetic or man-made stone rather than the lovely natural creation that it is. Perhaps this is because they are frequently, if not usually, treated.

Zircons are regularly treated to alter color, as in the blue and colorless zircons so often seen (many might mistake the colorless zircon for diamond because of its strong brilliance), but zircons also occur naturally in yellow, brown, orange, and red.

Colorless zircons, because of their intense brilliance and very low cost, offer an interesting alternative to diamonds as a stone to offset or dress up colored stones. But care needs to be exercised because zircon is brittle and will chip or abrade easily. For this reason, zircon is recommended for earrings, pendants, brooches, or rings with a protective setting.

Zoisite (Tanzanite)

Zoisite was not considered a gem material until 1967, when a beautiful, rich, blue to purple blue, transparent variety was found in Tanzania (hence tanzanite). Tanzanite can possess a rich, sapphire blue color (possibly with some violet red or greenish yellow flashes).

This lovely gem can cost over $2,000 per carat today in larger sizes. But one must be cautious. It is relatively soft, so we do not recommend tanzanite for rings (unless it's set in a *very* protected setting) or for everyday wear in which it would be exposed to knocks and other abuse.

One must also be aware that a very inexpensive, dull, brownish zoisite can become a beautiful, expensive tanzanite after heat treatment. If you love the stone and desire a piece of tanzanite jewelry, the decision is yours, but remember its major shortcoming—it's fragile.

Part Four

Important Advice Before You Buy

17

How to Select
a Reputable Jeweler

It would be impossible for us to give any hard-and-fast rules on this matter since there are so many exceptions. Some one-man operations are very highly respected and others are real opportunists. Some well-established firms that have been in business for many years have built their trade on the highest standards of integrity and knowledge, and others should have been put out of business years ago.

One point worth stressing is that for the average consumer, price will not be a reliable guide as any indicator of integrity or knowledge. Aside from the basic differences in quality, which will usually not be readily discernible to the consumer, there are cost differences resulting from the process by which the jewelry is manufactured. There are many jewelry manufacturers selling mass-produced lines of good-quality jewelry to jewelers all across the country. Mass-produced items, many of which are beautiful, classic designs (and sometimes knockoffs of a famous designer), are usually cheaper. Then there are the designers who create unique pieces or limited quantities of their designs, which are available in only a few select establishments. A premium is always paid for handmade or one-of-a-kind pieces, since the initial cost of production is being paid by one individual rather than being amortized across many.

And jewelers do not all work from the same markup. Markup depends upon operating costs and credit risks, among other things.

The best way to select is through shopping around. Take the time to look, compare merchandise, quality, design, and ask questions. As part of this process, it may be helpful to consider the following:

How long has the firm been in business? If it is an established firm, a quick check with the Better Business Bureau may reveal consumer complaints.

What are the credentials of the jeweler, manager, or owner?

How would you describe the store window? A window of jewelry nicely displayed? Or alluring bargains and come-on advertising to lure you in?

How would you describe the overall atmosphere? Professional, helpful, tasteful? Or hustling, pushy, intimidating?

What is their policy regarding returns? Will they allow a piece to be taken "on memo" (this is increasingly unusual today—too many jewelers have been ripped off)? To what extent will they guarantee their merchandise to be as represented? Be careful here. Make sure you've asked the right questions and have the right information on the bill of sale, or you may find yourself stuck because of a technicality. If they refuse to provide the necessary information, forget it and go to another jeweler. *Never allow yourself to be intimidated into "trusting them."* A trustworthy jeweler will have no problem giving you the information you request—in writing. And be sure that if you are making the purchase on a contingent basis the terms of the contingency are on the bill of sale.

What is their repair or replacement policy?

Never purchase fine, expensive gems through the mail.

Again, in general, you will be in a stronger position to differentiate between a knowledgeable, reputable jeweler and one who isn't if you've shopped around first. Unless you are an expert, visit several firms, ask questions, and then you be the judge.

18

How to Select a Reputable Gemologist-Appraiser

Why Get an Appraisal?

Obtaining an appraisal on a fine gem, and keeping it updated, is essential today for the following reasons:

1. For verification of the facts as represented by the seller (prior to purchase or immediately thereafter).
2. To obtain adequate insurance to protect against theft, loss, or damage.
3. To provide positive identification of *your* property where stolen property has been recovered.
4. To provide a complete description to ensure satisfactory replacement of a stolen, lost, or damaged piece.

The growing concern over the world money market and inflation has encouraged many people to put their savings or investment money into the "safety" of gem investment, resulting in an increase in the availability of jewelry to the buyer from questionable sources that use questionable trade practices and incentives, and specialize in mediocre merchandise. These may include certain types of discount houses (some of which are not really discounting at all), catalog showrooms, some wholesalers, the small operator selling through the news media, the private seller who "needs cash," the John Doe wishing to sell his inheritance, or the weekend exhibition/sale at local hotels, complete with free drinks. Certainly, if one is considering a purchase from any of the above sources, it should become obvious immediately why an intelligent buyer would find it essential to seek an appraisal first.

The need for appraisal services has also increased greatly because of the increase in theft, and the very sharp increase in the prices of diamonds and colored gems. It has become a necessity in these times to have any fine gem properly appraised, particularly prior to making a purchase decision, given today's costs and the potential for loss if the gem is not accurately represented.

It is also important, given the recent dramatic increase in gem prices, to update value estimations from old appraisals to ensure adequate coverage in the event of theft of gems that have been in your possession for several years or more. In addition, appraisals may be needed for inheritance taxes, gifts, or in the determination of your net worth.

How to Find a Reliable Appraiser

The appraisal business has been a booming business in the past few years. Many jewelry firms have begun to provide appraisal services. We must point out, however, that there are essentially no established guidelines for gem appraising, and almost anyone can represent himself as an appraiser. While there are many highly qualified professionals, there are also many who lack the expertise to offer these services. So it is essential that you select the appraiser with care and diligence. Further, if the purpose of the appraisal is to verify a gem and its value, we recommend that one deal only with an unbiased professional who is in the business of gem identification and appraising and *not* in the primary business of selling gems himself.

Most consumers do not know where or how to find a qualified gemologist-appraiser. The following should be helpful:

Check for local lists of professional associations and clubs. Contact the association or club president to see if he can make any recommendations. The Yellow Pages will provide names, but you must check them carefully following the suggestions given in this section.

Check the "Sources for Additional Information" for a list of gem-identifica-

tion laboratories (page 193) to find out if they do full appraisals for the consumer. Some do. If they do not, they may make a recommendation.

Obtain several names and then check the appraisers' credentials. To be a qualified gemologist-appraiser requires extensive formal training and experience. A preliminary credentials check can be conducted by telephone. The Gemological Institute of America and the Gemmological Association of Great Britain provide internationally recognized diplomas. G.I.A.'s highest award is G.G. (Graduate Gemologist) and the Gemmological Association of Great Britain awards the F.G.A. (Fellow of the Gemmological Association—and there are some who hold this honor "With Distinction"). Make sure the appraiser you select has one of these diplomas. Where possible, look for the title "Certified Gemologist Appraiser" (awarded by the American Gem Society), or "Master Gemologist Appraiser" (awarded by the American Society of Appraisers). These are currently the highest awards presented to jewelry appraisers.

Check the appraiser's length of experience. This can also be done on the telephone. In addition to formal training, a gemologist-appraiser needs extensive experience in the handling of gems, the use of the equipment necessary for accurate identification and evaluation, and activity in the marketplace, particularly today, with such strong price fluctuations. It is recommended that he have at least several years' experience in a well-equipped laboratory. If the gem being appraised is a colored gem, the complexities are much greater and require much more extensive experience.

Ask where the appraisal will be conducted. An appraisal should normally be done in the presence of the customer, if possible. This is important in order to ensure that the same stone is returned to you *and* to protect the appraiser. Recently we appraised an old platinum engagement ring that had over twenty years' filth compacted under the high, filigree-type box mounting typical of the early 1920s. After cleaning, which was difficult, the diamond showed a definite brown tint, easily seen by the client, which she had never noticed when the ring was dirty. She had just inherited the ring from her deceased mother-in-law, who had told her it had a blue white color. If she had not been present when this ring was being cleaned and appraised, it might have resulted in a lawsuit, for she would certainly have suspected a switch. This particular situation does not present itself often, but the appraiser must always be careful not to chip, change, or damage the item entrusted to him; and the customer must be equally alert to make sure that he does not. This can be very time-consuming if several pieces are being appraised. It normally takes about ½ hour per item to get all of the speci-fications, and it can take much longer in some cases.

Ask what type of equipment the appraiser uses to conduct an appraisal. Here is a list of equipment necessary to properly appraise gems. No prop-erly equipped lab should be without any of these items:

- The Leveridge Diamond and Millimeter Gauge, for measuring stones to estimate their approximate weight
- A plastic millimeter scale, 6 to 12 inches long, for measuring bracelets, etc.
- A microscope, GIA type, such as the Mark V Deluxe, complete with a diamond-grader attachment for color comparison or grading; a diamond proportion analyzer eyepiece; an overhead fluorescent light source; a Bausch & Lomb vertical illuminator to facilitate observing pinpoint, reflector-type inclusions; a measuring eyepiece (Filar eyepiece)
- A long-wave and short-wave ultraviolet lamp for stones whose fluorescence can be used as a means of identification
- A spectroscope (such as the model #808 supplied by the GIA to determine whether a stone's color is natural or artificially in-duced)
- A headpiece magnifier or suitable magnifier to use in conjunc-tion with a fine spread gauge
- An accurate balance scale for weighing loose stones
- A good desk lamp with a nonglare daylight-type illumination
- A good 10X corrected loupe, such as the B and L Hastings Triplet
- A dichroscope
- A Chelsea filter
- A polariscope
- A refractometer
- A beaker or glass full of clean isopropyl (rubbing) alcohol for examining stones wet, which enables the appraiser to look into most stones more easily
- A good set of specific-gravity liquids
- A color-graded set of master stones to determine color grade, a must for most diamond appraisers past fifty years of age

Optional Equipment

- A GIA Conductometer for testing the electrical conductivity
- A GIA Proportionscope

- A GIA Photoscope to take photographs of unusual inclusions
- A GIA Photostand or Polaroid CU-5 camera with attachments to photograph unusual pieces of jewelry
- A GIA Colormaster

The goal of the professional gemologist-appraiser is to completely document the customer's stone or piece of jewelry. Check to see what is being examined and evaluated. The following discussion will provide a guide to the pertinent data that should be included in the appraisal. Should an appraiser not have the equipment or expertise to provide the data, go to another appraiser.

Diamonds

A complete diamond appraisal should include the following information:

Size. Approximate or exact *carat weight and millimeter dimensions.* Loose (unmounted) stones should be weighed on an accurate balance scale. An appraiser can closely estimate the weight of mounted stones by using a Leveridge Diamond Gauge. *In addition to carat weight, millimeter dimensions are essential for future positive identification on stones over ½ carat.* Be sure the appraiser has included the millimeter dimension of the length, width, and depth, depending upon the shape of the stone. Width and depth are sufficient for round stones; length, width, and depth are needed for fancy cuts.

Color. The appraiser should indicate the color grade using a recognized, accepted color-grading system, such as the GIA scale, which ranks color with an alphabet letter ranging from D, the finest possible, down to Z. You should note here that he should grade color by comparing your stone to master stones for classification. This is a good practice for any appraiser, especially for persons past the age of fifty, since the vitreous matter in the eyeball tends to discolor and become somewhat yellowed itself, which will make certain slightly off-color stones look better to the older viewer than they actually are.

Flawlessness. The appraiser should grade flawlessness (clarity) with the microscope, at 10X magnification *only,* although some appraisers do prefer to use the hand loupe. The loupe will enable the appraiser to examine the stone without the interference of the stone-holder tongs on the microscope.

Some appraisers indicate the type and the location of the imperfections on a black and white schematic attached to, or incorporated in, the appraisal. The GIA flaw classification is the most frequently used, but other systems may be used. Have the appraiser stipulate which classification he is using. Note: Terms such as *commercially perfect* are in violation of FTC rulings.

Cut/Proportion. The appraiser should indicate the *shape* (round, emerald cut, fancy, etc.), note the quality of the *proportioning*, state the quality of the *finish*, and indicate the depth percentage (the ratio of the width to the depth).

Fluorescence. The use of long-wave, ultraviolet light will often indicate if the stone is fluorescent and, if so, whether weakly or strongly. It will also show the color of the fluorescence. Fluorescence can be a great aid in the identification of jewelry set with numerous diamonds. Taking a photograph (usually for a nominal additional charge) under normal conditions, and another photo using the same camera setup but with ultraviolet light in place of the normal white light, makes a permanent record or "fingerprint" of the fluorescent diamonds. This record can be used to positively identify a piece that may have been stolen, and to check for fraudulent substitution.

Electrical conductivity. Although most diamonds are not electrically conductive (except for natural blue stones), the GIA Conductometer may detect a conducting stone, which may help to positively identify a particular diamond if there is suspicion of substitution. A good appraiser should, therefore, include this test.

Spectroscopic examination. This is a mandatory examination for fancy colored diamonds to determine whether the stone is naturally or artificially colored. A good appraiser should *always* conduct this test on a colored diamond.

Colored Gems

A good gemologist will examine the stone for this information in the appraisal:

Identity. Species (spinel, amethyst, sapphire, etc.) and whether genuine, synthetic, composite, or simulated.

Size. Size and shape in millimeters; exact weight in carats, if unmounted, and estimated carat weight if mounted.

Color. The *hue* (spectral color—blue, red, green, etc.) will be stated. Also, the *intensity* (strong or weak), *tone* (light, dark) *evenness of color* (even and pure, color-zoned, patchy, uneven). Is the color *natural?* If not, it should be noted whether color is due to irradiation or other treatment. Does the *color change* (alexandrite-like)? The color classification according to the GIA Colormaster should also be indicated.

Fluorescent response under ultraviolet radiation.

Settings

Kind of metal. Gold, platinum, sterling, etc.. *Fineness* of metal—14K or 585; 18K or 750, etc.

Color. Two- or three-toned fabrication; white, yellow, pink.

Workmanship. Handmade, cast, die-struck; proportioning; finishing; soldering; pinholes; cracks; missing prongs or beads. Rate as excellent, good, or poor.

Sizes. Approximate millimeter sizes and shapes of brooches, pendants, charms, etc.

Types of catches. Safety chains, tongue-and-groove, spring ring, etc.

Types of chains. Foxtail, cable, twisted rope, long and short, figaro, Boston link, etc.

Type of box. Bezel set, belcher, prong, channel, fishtail, miracle, plate, bead set, tube set, etc.

Appraising Antique Jewelry

This is far more difficult, and sometimes impossible, unless it is the appraiser's area of specialization.

The appraisal is based on an evaluation of the precious metal and stone content at current prices, but the following data must also be considered before reaching the final valuation:

- Beauty and desirability
- Quality of the workmanship—handmade, cast, sculptured, chased, etc.
- Amount of wear and tear
- Period authenticity
- Rarity

In addition, a piece of jewelry that has been associated with some notable person, or designed by some famous artisan (such as Fabergé or I. Schorr), will have increased desirability and, therefore, value, and *the artisan must be noted on the appraisal.*

Appraisal Fees

This is a touchy and complex subject. Any appraisal should be done in writing, and accompanied by a suitable charge. Fees should be conspicuously posted so that the customer knows beforehand what he can expect to pay for this service.

Fees are essentially based on the expertise of the appraiser and the time involved (including secretarial work). While it used to be standard practice to base appraisal fees on a percentage of the appraised value, this practice is no longer acceptable. Today, all recognized appraisal associations in the United States recommend that fees be based on a flat hourly rate, or on a "per carat" charge for diamonds.

There is usually a minimum appraisal fee, regardless of value. The hourly rate charged by a professional, experienced gemologist–appraiser can range from $50 to $150, depending upon the complexity of the work to be performed and the degree of expertise required. Find out beforehand what the hourly rate is and what the minimum fee will be.

For multiple-item appraisals, special arrangements are usually made. For appraisals containing many items, such as an estate appraisal, an hourly rate of $50 to $75 is normal. Extra services, such as photography, X-radiography, Gemprint, or spectroscopic examination of fancy colored diamonds, will require additional fees.

Be wary of appraisal services offering appraisals at cheap rates, and of appraisers who continue to base their fee on a percentage of the "appraised valuation." The Internal Revenue Service will not accept appraisals performed by appraisers who charge a "percentage-based" fee.

Mr. Bonanno usually takes a photograph of the piece he is appraising (except for simple watches and simple rings). On the photograph he notes the approximate magnification, the date, and the owner's name, and he signs it using his personalized embossing seal to make an impression over his name. This provides a means of identifying merchandise that may have been stolen, damaged, etc., and will also aid in duplicating the piece should the customer so desire. The photograph may also be used for the U.S. Customs Service should the customer be a world traveler.

With the information provided here, the consumer will know how to evaluate the appraiser and ensure that accurate, *complete* documentation is provided.

19

A Word About Investment

Caution!

Caution is the only word we can apply to gem investment. More than two hundred gem-investment companies have been organized since the mid-1970s. NYDEX (New York Diamond Exchange) incorporated Wall Street techniques with New York's diamond district. Gems have played a role in formal retirement plans (which are presently not permitted, but may be again in the not-too-distant future). Merrill Lynch has organized a special division to handle such investment. Etc. But in one year, a year when diamond prices *doubled*, investors were duped out of an estimated $100,000,000! And as the potential market grows, so does the risk that one may fall prey to a fraudulent schemer.

If you have taken the time to read any of this book, you should now fully understand that the world of gems is very complex, that fraud and misrepresentation can be costly, and that the average consumer lacks the knowledge and experience to make sound judgments on the purchase of expensive gems without the assistance of a qualified gemologist-appraiser.

It is for this reason primarily that we recommend that gems and jewelry be purchased first and foremost for the pleasure they will bring to the purchaser/wearer, or as something to be handed down to future generations. The investment consideration, while it is certainly a valid consideration, in most cases should remain secondary.

However, if you can't resist the temptation of gem investment, and if a contemplated investment can be professionally evaluated before you close the deal, it may have merit. There are certainly some strong facts to support gem investment . . .

Some Facts in Support of Gem Investment

Over a five-year period, gem prices have increased significantly for both precious and semiprecious stones. While the finest-quality diamonds in 1-carat sizes and up suffered a severe decline in late 1980–early 1981 (after an unprecedented appreciation from 1978 to 1980), on an average basis diamonds were still a very sound investment, and smaller diamonds of very good quality, and stones of good quality generally, held very well even during the decline of the finest-quality larger stones.

Salomon Brothers (investment company) reported that rough (uncut) diamonds had appreciated at a compounded rate of 14.5 percent a year for the past ten years, 16.9 percent for the past five years, and had stayed even for the twelve-month period ending June 1981. For the five- and 10-year periods, diamonds as investments ranked ahead of bonds, housing, and the government's Consumer Price Index. For the 12-month period, while farmland and oil were better investments than diamonds, diamonds outperformed investments in gold, silver, bonds, U.S. coins, and foreign exchange.

Gems can be used and enjoyed without adversely affecting value, unlike most other beautiful things people buy and use (autos, furs, furniture, etc.)

Historically, there has always been a market for gems. Good stones are not trendy and don't go in and out of fashion, like some fine-art investments, where an artist is popular today and never heard of in a few years.

Gems have portability—they are easily moved and stored, so they are readily available to the owner, easy to show when the need arises.

Some Facts That May Discourage
Gem Investment

Extreme care must be taken to verify the authenticity of the gem being considered and to determine its precise quality/value. For this reason we advise against consideration of sealed merchandise.

Gems are not a short-term investment. In most cases, depending upon the price you have paid (the average consumer buys at retail, not at wholesale) and the rate of appreciation, there is a minimum five-year period simply to break even.

Liquidity can be a problem. Since you are not a jeweler, your own credibility will be suspect where the average consumer is concerned, so it may be very difficult to find a buyer for your gem.

Jewelers may be interested in buying "off the street," but the seller usually gets less than the current wholesale price in such transactions. This is not because the jeweler is trying to take advantage so much as a matter of simple economics. When the jeweler has a customer for a specific piece, he can always go to his dealer to obtain what he needs. Not only does he not risk tying up his money until he actually has a customer, but he may also charge the cost to his account and carry his cost for an extra thirty days or more, earning that extra interest on the money in the bank. Therefore, the only incentive for him to tie his money up in a cash transaction off the street, for which he may or may not even have an immediate customer, is if the price is attractive enough—usually *half the wholesale cost.* Yet another consideration is his own protection—he has no way to determine whether merchandise bought off the street is stolen property, which could end up confiscated by police (in which case he loses whatever he paid for the goods). There may be exceptions made if the piece is particularly fine or rare or unusual in some way, but the norm is as stated above.

Investment-house buy-back guarantees are *no* guarantee. Some of the new investment firms guarantee buy-back after a prescribed time period. Unfortunately, you have no way of knowing where they will be after the prescribed period of time—whether they will still be in business, or how solvent they might remain in a period of economic unrest if, for example, everyone decided to take them up on their guarantee at the same time.

The major concern is the liquidity problem. Some jewelers and legitimate investment firms have conscientiously attempted to help alleviate concern over this problem. Some offer to buy back at 90 percent of the current retail value any stone they've sold—at any time. This kind of policy certainly has allure and seems to reduce the risk.

Others have made arrangements with local banks to lend up to 70 percent of the value of diamonds sold by them, to enable the investor to raise quick cash on the diamonds without having to sell them. This is very innovative marketing . . . but only time will tell how effective.

A Few Investment Observations

One Carat and Up Diamonds versus Smaller Diamonds

While the emphasis in diamond investment has been on stones of 1 carat and up, the steadiest and most continuous growth has been with stones of very fine quality in the ½-carat and ¾-carat sizes. As prices for stones of 1 carat and up became prohibitive, there was a major shift among consumers to smaller sizes. (Engagement ring styles also began to shift to multistone rings containing two or more smaller stones in place of one large solitaire.) Good to very good stones of 1 to 2 carats will be a good investment. At the same time, they might be more difficult to sell or liquidate.

The Fancy Diamond Market

Colored natural diamonds still offer outstanding opportunity. The canary, as well as certain other pastel shades, in the finest of qualities is still selling for less than the finest colorless diamonds, except possibly in the case of fine pink fancies. And the brown, which sells for perhaps less per carat than any other of the fancy varieties, is quite an interesting stone with tremendous fashion versatility and appreciation potential.

Furthermore, availability of these fancy colored diamonds may be greater at this time than at any other time in recent history, or than it may be again for many years, due, we've been told, to the presence of numerous Iranian stones placed on the market by post-Shah Iranian leaders.

Sapphire, Ruby, and Emerald

These are also good stones to consider for investment. Fine-quality stones in sizes over 2 carats are becoming more and more scarce, but there will always be a market for these most precious of precious stones. Ideally, investment stones in this group should be at least 1½ carats, but once again, ¾-carat to 1-carat stones have shown significant appreciation, as with the smaller diamonds, so they should not be ignored if the quality is outstanding. (Note: There has been a tendency recently to overprice rubies at the wholesale level, and buyer resistance has therefore become greater.)

Semiprecious Stones

As a general rule today you can almost bet that semiprecious stones that approximate ruby, sapphire, and emerald in color, and possess a nice brilliance and good durability, will appreciate dramatically in value, as was seen in 1980–81. Good examples of this appreciation can be seen in rubellite (pink to red tourmaline), tanzanite, and tsavorite (green garnet). Aquamarine has also shown pronounced appreciation. Check the colored gemstone chart (page 127) for other good prospects.

Good investment size in this group is hard to state. Generally, the larger the better. One can find nice rubellite in sizes over 5 carats, but tsavorite over 5 carats is rare.

Gem Investment in Summary

All in all, a strong case can be made for either side of the investment question. Innovative marketing has opened the doors on some interesting investment options in gems, and there is an increasing number of qualified gemologists to provide sound consultation. And we hope this book has also taken some of the mystery away and provided some healthy insights that will make a difference at least for you. Perhaps the nicest part of gem investment is that it can provide a nice, convenient rationalization for a lovely jewelry purchase. With a gem investment you actually have something beautiful that you can personally enjoy whether or not it turns out to have been the "wisest" investment.

But we cannot stress too strongly the following:

- Exercise caution and remember, *there is usually no such thing as a bargain.*
- It is essential to deal with reputable firms that can be thoroughly investigated . . . and that you *have* investigated.

- No matter who the person is with whom you are dealing, no matter how reputable the firm, *never* enter into any gem investment without expert consultation with a qualified gemologist-appraiser to verify the authenticity, quality, and actual current *wholesale* and *retail* value of the merchandise.

And in final summary . . . Remember, as a rule, *You get no bargains in gems. You get only what you pay for . . . or less.*

Sources for Additional Information

A Selected List of Gem-Identification Laboratories

These larger labs have been listed for your convenience. Please check Yellow Pages for a complete listing in your area, and follow our suggestions in Chapter 18. Keep in mind that not all labs will put a dollar value on the stone.

American Gemological Laboratory
580 Fifth Ave.
New York, NY 10036

European Gemological Laboratory
608 S. Hill St., Ste. 1013
Los Angeles, CA 90014

Gemological Appraisal Association
666 Washington Road
Pittsburgh, PA 15228

GIA Gem Trade Laboratory
580 Fifth Ave.
New York, NY 10036

Gemological Institute of America
1660 Stewart St.
Santa Monica, CA 90404

International Gemmological Institute
580 Fifth Ave.
New York, NY 10036

National Gem Appraising Lab.
8600 Fenton St.
Silver Spring, MD 20910

Joseph Tenhagen, Inc.
36 NE First St.
Miami, FL 33132

Some of these labs also offer courses in gemology that you might find interesting and informative. They vary significantly in cost, level, number of hours, residency requirements, and the like. For special information, contact lab.

National Jewelry Associations

Accredited Gemologists Assoc.
Office of Publications
1615 South Foothill Drive
Salt Lake City, Utah 84108
(801) 581-9900 or 364-3667
Dana Richardson, Editor

Organization of gemologists awarded the AGA certificate to help individuals identify trustworthy, capable gemologists. Accredits laboratories, publishes newsletter, sponsors educational programs and gemological research, polices members, and works with officials to advocate policies beneficial to industry.

American Gem Society
2960 Wilshire Blvd.
Los Angeles, CA 90010
(213) 387-7375
Alfred L. Woodill,
   Executive Director

AGS is a nonprofit, professional organization of jewelers in the United States and Canada. Its purpose: to advance gemological knowledge, foster ethical business practices, enhance the public image of the jewelry industry, and educate the consumer. A free consumer kit is available on request.

193

American Gem & Mineral Suppliers Association
1299 Armando St.
Upland, CA 91786
(714) 981-8588
Irene Elliot, Executive Secretary

Members are retailers, manufacturers, wholesalers, importers, distrib-
utors, or publishers in the gem,
mineral, lapidary, and allied fields.

American Gem Trade Association
World Trade Center, Suite 181
2050 Stemmons Expressway
Dallas, Texas 75207
(214) 742-4367 (800) 972-1162
Peggy Willett, Executive Director

An association representing the natural
colored gemstone industry in the U.S.
and Canada, dedicated to furthering
awareness and education about colored
gems, upholding high ethical standards
among members, and fighting fraud.
Promotional and educational materials,
and expert speakers, available.

American Society of Appraisers
Box 17265, Dulles International
  Airport
Washington, DC 20041
(703) 478-2228
Shirley Belz,
  Public Relations Director

Created in 1952 by a merger of two associations. It administers the prestigious
Master Gemologist Appraiser program
which tests, certifies, and polices gemologist appraisers desiring or holding the
"Master Gemologist Appraiser" title.
Publishes a journal, newsletters, mon-
ographs, and an appraisal manual, and
a multidisciplinary *Bibliography of Appraisal Literature*. Sponsors conferences,
seminars, workshops, consumer information programs, and provides free
pamphlets and brochures to the public.
Initiator/sponsor of the Valuation Sci-
ences Degree Program in colleges and
universities throughout the country.

Appraisers Association
  of America, Inc.
60 East 42nd St.
New York, NY 10165
(212) 867-9775
Victor Wiener, Executive Director

A group of over 1,200 appraisers in a
variety of fields. Its purpose: to establish
and maintain ethical standards, to improve appraisal skills, and to publicize
the profession.

Canadian Jewellers Association
1491 Yonge St.
Toronto, Ont. M4T 124, Canada
(416) 922-9901
Laurence K. Marans, President
David M. Dore, General Manager

Represents Canadian jewelers in
business and government. Sponsors annual trade shows.

Canadian Jewellers Institute
1491 Yonge St.
Toronto, Ont. M4T 124, Canada
(416) 922-9901
David M. Dore, General Manager

Offers Retail Jewelers Training Course leading to G. J. (Graduate Jeweler) and various seminar programs for Canadian jewelers at all levels. Publishes textbook, *Jewellery Today.*

CIBJO—Confedorafi Lungotevere
  degli Araguillara
00153—Roma, Italia
M. Raffaele Amirante, President
Dr. Crescenzo Gatti, Secretary

Founded in 1961 to coordinate the work of independent national trade organizations of manufacturers, wholesalers, stone dealers, and retailers and harmonize trade practices in such matters as quality standards for precious metals and gemstone nomenclature. Members: Austria, Belgium, Canada, Denmark, Finland, France, Great Britain, Italy, Japan, Netherlands, Norway, Spain, Sweden, Switzerland, United States, and West Germany.

Diamond Council of America, Inc.
250 Hammond Pond Pkwy.,
  Suite 1702N
Chestnut Hill, MA 02167
(617) 965-0320
Myer B. Barr, Executive Director

DCA offers courses in "diamontology" and gemology to employees of member firms. Council supplies advertising and educational materials to members. Membership includes firms from all fifty states, Canada, Australia, India, and Africa. Dr. Arthur H. Brownlow, Chairman of Geology of Boston University, supervises home-study courses for over 2,000 employee-students annually and over 1,100 jewelry store members. Scientific technology as well as salesmanship and merchandising is emphasized. DCA is a nonprofit educational foundation.

Diamond Dealers Club Inc.
30 West 47th St.
Diamond Club Bldg.
New York, NY 10036
(212) 719-4321
Abe Shainberg, Executive Director
  and Attorney

Affiliated with World Federation of Diamond Bourses. Founded in 1931, has 2,100 members. The Club works to eliminate abuses and unfair trade practices in the diamond industry and keeps members informed of important trade happenings.

International Colored Gemstone
  Association, Inc.
22643 Strathern St.,
West Hills, CA 91304
(818) 716-0489
Maureen E. Jones, Executive
  Director

Nonprofit organization of gem-stone miners, cutters, and whole-salers from 34 countries, working to build closer cooperation in the gemstone trade and develop a common language and consistent standards. Its "Gembureau" pro-motes the understanding and appreciation of gemstones.

Jewelers of America, Inc.
1271 Avenue of the Americas
New York, NY 10020
(212) 489-0023
Michael D. Roman, Chairman and
  Executive Director
Legislative Office:
  1725 DeSales St. NW
Washington, DC 20036
(202) 628-3355

JA is the nationwide trade associa-tion dedicated to promoting the welfare of all retail jewelers. The association offers benefits, services, and educational programs specifi-cally designed to aid its jeweler-members in their retail operations. JA now has a national consumer information program offering free brochures giving guidelines for buying fine jewelry as well as in-formation on products, trends, and experts' advice on all aspects of fine jewelry.

National Association of Jewelry
  Appraisers
4210 North Brown Avenue, Suite "A"
Scottsdale, AZ 85251
(602) 941-8088
Richard E. Baron, Executive Director

The National Association of Jewelry Appraisers is the largest international association which performs gem and jewelry valuation exclusively. It is dedicated to developing and main-taining professional standards for jewelry appraising. A free member directory, indicating areas of spe-cialization/expertise, is available on request.

Precious Metals Institute
5 Mechanic St.
Attleboro, MA 02703
(617) 222-3666
S. L. Cantor, Executive Director

Service covers general industrial and public information regarding all silver, gold, and platinum prod-ucts, including bi- or tri-metals.

State Jewelers' Associations

Alabama Jewelers Association, Inc.
22 Wood Manor
Tuscaloosa, AL 35401
(205) 759-1326
Paul Vining, Executive Director

Arizona Jewelers Association
P. O. Box. 34125
Phoenix, AZ 85067
Robert B. Westover,
  Executive Director

California Jewelers Association
606 S. Olive St., Suite 714
Los Angeles, CA 90014
(213) 628-3171
Elva Pascoe, Executive Director

Colorado and Eastern Wyoming,
  Rocky Mountain Jewelers Asso-
  ciation
P.O. Box 24105
Denver, CO 80224
(303) 757-2134
Helen Sherer, Executive Secretary

Connecticut Jewelers Association
179 Allyn St., Suite 304
Hartford, CT 06103
(203) 246-6566
Edward Isenberg, Permanent Executive Secretary

Florida Jewelers Association
1940 Buford Blvd.
Tallahassee, FL 32317
(904) 878-3134
Robert S. Rhinehart, Jr.,
  Executive Director

Georgia Jewelers Association
P.O. Box 801
Macon, GA 31202
(912) 743-8612
Joe Andrews, Executive Secretary

Hawaii Jewelers Association
P.O. Box 513
Honolulu, HI 96809
(808) 395-2866
Ann Marceau, Executive Director

Illinois Jewelers Association
2021 Barberry Dr.
Springfield, IL 62704
(212) 546-0532
Executive Secretary

Indiana Jewelers Association
Illinois Bldg.
17 W. Market St., Suite 321
P.O. Box 2104
Indianapolis, IN 46206
(317) 631-8124
Normagene S. Murray,
  Executive Secretary

Intermountain Retail Jewelers
  Association, Inc.
c/o Gem Jewelers
152 N. Main St.
Cedar City, UT 84720
(801) 586-8464
Vernal Taysom, President

Iowa Jewelers and Watchmakers
  Association
906 S.W. Second St.
Eagle Grove, IA 50533
(515) 448-4640
Lillian Lockes, Executive Director

Kentucky Jewelers Association
17 W. Market St., Suite 610
P.O. Box 2104
Indianapolis, IN 46206
(317) 631-8124
Normagene S. Murray,
   Executive Secretary

Louisiana, Jewelers of, Inc.
P.O. Box 41
Kentwood, LA 70444
(504) 229-2810
William Morris, Executive Director

Marine Retail Jewelers Association
c/o Carter Brothers Co.
521 Congress St.
Portland, ME 04101
(207) 773-0291
Normand M. Moreau

Maryland–Delaware–District of
   Columbia Jewelers Association
3635 Old Court Rd., Suite 210
Baltimore, MD 21208
(301) 484-6770
Frances Goodman,
   Executive Secretary

Massachusetts–Rhode Island Jewelers Association
c/o Hingham Jewelers
54 South St.
Hingham, MA 02043
(617) 749-2108
Angelo A. Manjos, President

Michigan Jewelers Association
211 N. Pine St.
Lansing, MI 48933
(517) 372-5656
Larry L. Meyer,
   Executive Vice-President

Minnesota Jewelers Association
2353 N. Rice St., Suite 220
Roseville, MN 55113
(612) 483-5264
Viva Thistlethwaite,
   Executive Director

Montana-Wyoming Jewelers Asso-
   ciation
P.O. Box 2276
Billings, MT 59103
(406) 259-7500
Dan Robinson, President
Frederick J. Nelson,
   Executive Vice-President

New Hampshire Retail Jewelers
   Association
c/o Cardin's Jewelers
107 W. Pearl St.
Nashua, NH 03060
(603) 889-0011
Richard A. Cardin, President

New Jersey Jewelers Association
24 W. Lafayette St.
Trenton, NJ 08608
(609) 393-8005
Richard M. Brandys, Director

New Mexico Jewelers Association
3122 Central SE
Albuquerque, NM 87106
(505) 255-3090
Beverly Martinez, President
Iona Beauchamp, Secretary

New York, Consolidated Retail
   Jewelers Association of Greater,
   Inc.
95 Jackson Ave.
Syosset, NY 11791
(516) 921-8760
Fay Ascher, Executive Secretary

New York State Retail Jewelers
Association
250 State St.
Albany, NY 12210
(518) 465-7878
Carol Buenau, Executive Secretary

North Carolina Jewelers
Association
c/o Green's Jewelers, Inc.
320 Market St.
Smithfield, NC 27577
(919) 934-5006
Jimmy Green, President

Ohio Jewelers Association
50 W. Broad St.
Columbus, OH 43215
(614) 221-7833
Jon B. Hurst, Executive Secretary

Oklahoma Jewelers Association,
  Inc.
P.O. Box 52753
Tulsa, OK 74152
(918) 663-3399 or (918) 622-2220
Alnoma E. Dinger,
  Executive Director

Oregon State Jewelers Association
919 S.W. Taylor St., #203
Portland, OR 97205
(503) 223-8772
Frank Breall, Executive Secretary

Pacific Northwest Jewelers Association
1500 E. Galer
Seattle, WA 98112
(206) 323-3770
Hanna Reisner, Executive Director

Pennsylvania Jewelers Association
22 S. Third St.
Harrisburg, PA 17101
(717) 233-3254
Thomas Weyant, CAE,
  Executive Secretary

South Carolina Retail Jewelers Association
901 Front St.
Georgetown, SC 29440
(803) 546-5741 or (803) 546-0306
Marvadine Forehand,
  Executive Secretary

Tennessee Jewelers Association
P.O. Box 567
Cookeville, TN 38501
(615) 893-9162
Lee Tidwell, Executive Secretary

Texas Jewelers Association
504 W. 12th St.
Austin, TX 78701
(512) 472-8261
Michael R. Moore,
  Executive Director

Vermont Retail Jewelers
  Association
c/o Atkins & Gould
405–409 Main St.
Bennington, VT 05201
(802) 442-2122
Charles Gould, President

Virginia Jewelers Association
FNEB Bldg., Suite 1211
Roanoke, VA 24011
(703) 981-1103
Harold F. Jennings, Jr.,
  Executive Secretary

West Virginia Retail Jewelers Association
240 Capitol St., Suite 610
Charleston, WV 25301
(304) 342-1183
Paul McKown, Executive Director

Wisconsin Jewelers Association
30 W. Mifflin St.
Madison, WI 53703
(608) 257-3541
Mary C. Kaja, Executive Secretary

Selected Readings

Anderson, B. W. *Gem Testing*. London: Heywood & Co., 1971.

This book may be too technical for the amateur.

Arem, Joel E. *Color Encyclopedia of Gemstones*. New York: Van Nostrand, Reinhold, 1977.

Excellent color photography makes this book interesting for anyone, but it is of particular value for the gemologist.

Ball, S. H. *The Mining of Gems and Ornamental Stones by American Indians*. Washington, D.C.: Smithsonian Institution, Anthropological Papers No. 13, 1941.

———. *A Roman Book on Precious Stones*. Los Angeles: Gemological Institute of America, 1950.

A Roman Book on Precious Stones is very interesting from a historical perspective, especially for the knowledgeable student of gemology.

Bank, Hermann. *Precious Stones and Minerals*. New York: F. Warne, 1970.

This book is good for the beginner because it isn't too technical, and it has nice color plates.

Bauer, M. *Precious Stones*. Translated by L. J. Spencer. Rutland, Vt.: C. E. Tuttle Co., 1971.

A comprehensive book recommended for the advanced student.

Beigbeder, O. *Ivory*. London: Weidenfeld & Nicholson, 1965.

Bradford, E. *Four Centuries of European Jewelry*. London: Country Life, Ltd., 1967.

Bruton, E. *Diamonds*. 2nd Edition. London: Northwood, 1977.

An excellent, encyclopedic, well-illustrated book, good for both amateur and professional gemologist.

Budge, Sir E. A. Wallis. *Amulets & Talismans.* New Hyde Park, N.Y.: University Books, 1961.
Interesting lore and mythology.

Cavenago-Bignami Moneta, S. *Gemmologia.* Milan: Heopli, 1965.
One of the most extensive works on gems available. Excellent photography. Available in the Italian language only. Recommended for advanced students.

Chu, Arthur and Grace. *The Collector's Book of Jade.* New York: Crown, 1978.

Desautels, P. E. *Gems in the Smithsonian Institution.* Washington, D.C.: Smithsonian Institution (Pub. No. 4608), 1968.
Excellent color plates. Very interesting for anyone.

Evans, Joan. *A History of Jewelry 1100–1870.* London: Faber and Faber, 1953.
Especially interesting for the antique jewelry collector.

Gaal, R. A. P. *A Diamond Dictionary.* Los Angeles: Gemological Institute of America, 1977.

Geological Museum, London. *A Guide to the Collection of Gemstones.* London: Her Majesty's Stationery Office, 1950.
Nice color plates. Interesting for the beginner.

Gubelin, Edward. *Inclusions as a Means to Gemstone Identification.* Los Angeles: Gemological Institute of America, 1953.

———. *Internal World of Gemstones.* Woburn, Mass.: Butterworth, 1979.
Both are recommended for the serious student of gemology.

Gump, Richard. *Jade, Stone Of Heaven.* Garden City, N.Y.: Doubleday, 1962.
Fascinating for anyone who loves jade.

Holmes, M. *The Crown Jewels.* London: Her Majesty's Stationery Office, 1955.

James B. *Collecting Australian Gemstones.* Sydney: Murray, 1970.

Kunz, G. F. *The Curious Lore of Precious Stones.* Reprinted 1972, with *The Magic of Jewels and Charms.* New York: Dover Publications.

———. *Gems and Precious Stones of North America.* Reprinted 1968. New York: Dover Publications.
Very interesting for both beginner and advanced.

Leechman, F. *The Opal Book.* Sydney: Ure Smith, 1968.

Good book on opals for both beginners and advanced.

Legand, Jacques, et al. *Diamonds, Myth, Magic and Reality.* New York: Crown, 1980.

Beautifully illustrated, fascinating for the amateur and professional alike.

Liddicoat, R. T. *Handbook of Gem Identification.* Los Angeles: Gemological Institute of America, 1969.

Textbook for the student of gemology.

Matlins, Antoinette Leonard & Bonanno, A.C. *Gem Identification Made Easy: A Hands-On Guide to More Confident Buying and Selling.* So. Woodstock, Vt.: GemStone Press, 1989.

A non-technical book on the subject explaining what instruments you need—including three that are pocket-size—and how to use them to identify diamonds and colored gems and separate them from imitations and "look-alikes." Practical, easy to understand.

Nott, Stanley C. *Chinese Jade Throughout the Ages.* Rutland, Vt.: C. E. Tuttle, 1962.

Excellent book for the jade collector.

Pagel-Theisen, V. *Diamond Grading ABC.* New York: Rubin & Son, 1980.

Highly recommended for anyone in diamond sales.

Pough, F. H. *The Story of Gems and Semiprecious Stones.* New York: Harvey House, 1969.

Good for beginning and amateur gemologists.

Schumann, W. *Gemstones of the World.* Translated by E. Stern. New York: Sterling Publishing Co., 1977.

This book has superior color plates of all of the gem families and their different varieties and for this reason would be valuable to anyone interested in gems.

Shaub, B. M. *Treasures from the Earth.* New York: Crown, 1975.

Interesting illustrations.

Shipley, R. M. *Dictionary of Gems and Gemology.* Los Angeles: Gemological Institute of America, 1951.

For the student of gemology.

Sinkankas, John. *Emeralds & Other Beryls*. Philadelphia: Chilton & Co., 1982.

————. *Gem Cutting*. Princeton; D. Van Nostrand & Co., 1962.

————. *Gemstones of North America*. Princeton: D. Van Nostrand & Co., 1959. Interesting and well illustrated, but portions may be too technical for the amateur.

Spencer, L. J. *Key to Precious Stones*. London: Blockie & Co., 1959. Good for the beginning student of gemology.

Twining, Lord. *A History of the Crown Jewels of Europe*. London: Batsford, 1962.

Webster, R. *Gem Identification*. New York: Sterling Publishing, 1975.

————. *Gemologist's Compendium*. 5th Edition. London: Northwood, 1970.

————. *Gems*. London: Butterworth & Co., 1970.

————. *Gems in Jewelry*. London: Northwood, 1975.

————. *Practical Gemology*. 6th Edition. London: Northwood, 1976. All of the above are highly recommended for the serious student of gemology, especially *Gems*.

Williamson, G. C. *The Book of Amber*. London: Ernest Benn, Ltd., 1932.

Zucker, Benjamin. *Gems and Jewels: A Connoisseur's Guide*. New York: Thames and Hudson, Inc., 1984. A lavishly illustrated book on the history and use of principal gems and "great" gemstones of the world, giving fascinating historical facts and mythological tidbits as well as many examples of the jeweler's art from widely differing cultures.

Index

204